Whole Life Worship is biblical, prophetic an[...] Sam and Sara offer an important correctiv[...] church worship but this is far from an angry book. The writing is full of love and grace. I was quite defensive when I began to read, expecting 'our worship' to be attacked. I was won over. The biblical exegesis is brilliant, thorough and engaging. The tone is compassionate and the message is revolutionary, if we will only take it on board. You may not like all the practical suggestions but you will find the overwhelming majority both creative and helpful. A most important and helpful book.
Mike Pilavachi, Soul Survivor

There can be little that is more important in the church today than helping people to connect what they do when they gather at church (what we often call worship) with what they do when they 'scatter' to live their lives (which we ought to call worship). *Whole Life Worship* does what it promises – helping worshippers and their leaders to make those connections – so neither what we do in church nor what we do the rest of the week is undervalued. Along the way, it lays solid foundations of understanding and then builds on them with practicable ideas about what to do.

It does all this with a realistic understanding of what is going on in actual churches, reflecting the differences not only between denominations and networks but also within them. Not only does this make the book both usable and useful across a wide spectrum of traditions, it also enables those traditions and approaches to learn from one another. And it does all this in an accessible and invitational style. It's hard to think of any church that would not benefit from reading *Whole Life Worship* and applying its wisdom.
Mark Earey, Tutor in Liturgy and Worship, The Queen's Foundation, Birmingham

Sam and Sara Hargreaves give me hope that, even in the bright glare of the worship industry supermarket, hiding in the shade, there is organic, beautiful, holistic creativity serving the grassroots of the church. This essential book is dripping with hard-won, honest local wisdom.
Andy Flannagan, worship leader, songwriter and political campaigner

Over the past year, I have had at least two conversations with Christians who wondered if the effort expended preparing for worship services could be better spent in other types of ministry. I wish I'd had a copy of Sam and Sara's book at the time because it offers the perfect answer to that question. Both in theory and through a feast of creative examples, they demonstrate how a regular period of worship offers the perfect opportunity to consider, celebrate and prepare for the worship we offer on our frontlines, day by day.

I cannot recommend this book highly enough. And I plan to carry a copy in my bag, so I have something to offer the next time the question comes up!
Bob Hartman, bestselling author and storyteller

If you want to see the church inspired and equipped to serve God in all spheres of life, read *Whole Life Worship*. Packed with thoughtful provocation and practical innovation, this is a vital book for all those who lead in our churches.
Krish Kandiah, Founder and Director, Home for Good

Thank you Sam and Sara for this well-timed, well-written, hugely inspiring act of worship in your writing. It draws us closer to the heart and intentions of God for the whole world and for the whole week. Great job! We are blessed and mentored by you.
Geraldine Luce (Latty), worship leader, songwriter and lecturer, London School of Theology

In the first chapter, I found myself convicted by Sam and Sara's questions about worship patterns. As I read them back to a friend, tears began flowing down my cheeks. Their chapters on the foundation for worship so gently exposed the blind spots in our cultural view of worship, I found myself unable to defend against them. I managed to get to the practical ideas and found hope blossoming for all us normal, everyday people who are blessed to have a part in welcoming the King of the Universe into our whole world.

Every leader needs this book – and when I say 'leader', I mean every 'person' whom Jesus died for. We all play a part in leading church and should be well versed in worship where God meets, empowers and pours through us.
Peter Nevland, spoken-word artist, speaker and author of Exposing the Psalms

In *Whole Life Worship*, Sam and Sara Hargreaves give relevant and accessible worship ideas – undergirded by key theologians and Christian leaders – to enable corporate worship to engage all of life. This inspiring new book will help churches of all denominations to lead and plan worship that encourages Christian mission in everyday life.
Jeremy Perigo, lecturer and Director of Music and Worship Programmes, London School of Theology

Insightful observations, inspiring anecdotes and resourceful ideas coalesce to make this book a valuable contribution to the worship arena. The overriding theme is that worship should not be reduced to the act of singing in tune; rather, it's clearly communicated that worship is about your whole life, your daily patterns and practices, and your heart ambitions being in tune with the purposes and presence of a God who 'so loves the world'.

Our corporate expressions of worship should not be world-weary escapism but world-informing engagement. Constructively, Sam and Sara celebrate and connect our gathered expressions of worship to our daily work and living-it-out-in-the-world worship, expounding the vital synergy between them by twinning theological context with practical ideas on how to better link the two. This book will help us to evaluate and develop the various elements of our worship events / services / gatherings but, more than that, it will also help to fuel a cultural shift as we discover more fully how to live out our worship.
Sue Rinaldi, songwriter and worship co-ordinator. www.suerinaldi.net

This is such a helpful, well-thought-out, biblically sound and beautifully practical book. It reminds us that the worship hidden in every corner of our lives is what makes sense of the songs we sing when we gather together. It invites us to become 'whole-life' worshippers – those who don't simply lift up their song, but those who lay their lives down for the sake of the King and kingdom.
Kathryn Scott, songwriter, worship leader and Lead Pastor, Causeway Coast Vineyard Church

Just as when you meet Sam and Sara Hargreaves face to face, so it is reading this well-considered book – you are immediately struck with three invigorating blows: this devoted couple's personal passion for their subject material; their desire to be totally practical by ensuring that their own clear theory is immediately and readily applied to real life; and that always, in all they write, Sam and Sara are truly and evidently campaigning to build up Christ's church.

This book manages remarkably to be as wide ranging as it is detailed; as imaginative as it is comprehensive. It pioneers helpfully a path we can follow, picking up innumerable tips, insights and nuggets of practicable advice along the way. It inspires me to action and resolve along a guided and well-documented route. Bravo and thanks to Sam and Sara, who motivate, lead and inform us of where we need to go.
Noel Tredinnick, Director of Music, All Souls Orchestra

In the English language, we commonly use the term 'worship' to refer not only to a public event but also to a profound (often musical) expression of adoration, as well as to a more general life-long intention to love and serve God. Often these dimensions of worship can be conflated or confused, and our discourse can unwittingly imply that public worship services or intense praise songs complete the worship of God. This book offers a compelling vision of a richer, integrated worship and Christian life, along with several practicable suggestions for nurturing this ambition in local communities.
John D. Witvliet, Director, Calvin Institute of Christian Worship, Calvin College and Calvin Theological Seminary, Grand Rapids, Michigan, USA

Sam & Sara Hargreaves

Whole
Life
WORSHIP

Empowering disciples for the frontline

INTER-VARSITY PRESS
36 Causton Street, London SW1P 4ST, England
Email: ivp@ivpbooks.com
Website: www.ivpbooks.com

First published 2017

British Library Cataloguing-in-Publication Data
A catalogue record for this book is available from the British Library.

ISBN: 978-1-78359-511-2
eBook ISBN: 978-1-78359-512-9

Set in Dante 12/15 pt
Typeset in Great Britain by CRB Associates, Potterhanworth, Lincolnshire
Printed in Great Britain by Ashford Colour Press Ltd, Gosport, Hampshire

*Inter-Varsity Press publishes Christian books that are true to the Bible and that
communicate the gospel, develop discipleship and strengthen the church for its mission
in the world.*

*IVP originated within the Inter-Varsity Fellowship, now the Universities and Colleges
Christian Fellowship, a student movement connecting Christian Unions in universities
and colleges throughout Great Britain, and a member movement of the International
Fellowship of Evangelical Students. Website: www.uccf.org.uk. That historic association
is maintained, and all senior IVP staff and committee members subscribe to the UCCF
Basis of Faith.*

CONTENTS

ILLUSTRATIONS

Figures

Table

FOREWORD

This is a pioneer book.

It's a book about a vital question: how can our Sunday worship of the God and King of the universe not only express our wonder, praise and love for him but help us live our whole Monday-to-Saturday lives differently? This book addresses that question head-on and provides inspiration and ideas that can be used in a range of local church settings.

It's a book that we have needed for a long time.

I began leading worship in church twenty-seven years ago. Our musicians were two wonderful teenagers playing a violin and a cello. The cello was the lead instrument. My only qualification was enthusiasm; my limitations were clear for all to see. But we worshipped, and somehow, in ways that are beyond my understanding, I think God was pleased.

I was the pastor. In preparing services each week, my hope was that we would encounter God together as we worshipped. And in the week, I wanted to meet those worshippers in the course of their everyday lives, discovering what God might be doing in and through them as they taught children, did the washing, finalized accounts for the bowls club, performed MOT tests, wherever they might be in a normal week.

What I struggled with was to know how to connect the Sunday experience with the Monday reality. I needed people who could help. I needed people who were seasoned and experienced, who didn't need my church to become a clone of theirs, who were able to give me resources, ideas and encouragement to think about how to lead worship in my inner-city church at that point in its history with those particular people in attendance.

I wish this pioneering book had been written twenty-eight years ago.

Many of us are asking how our worship together helps us see our Monday-to-Saturday life through new eyes. We know this will not happen by adding a few tweaks to our existing practices. It will need a change in our church culture.

Sam and Sara have led worship in small churches, in large churches, at international conferences, and for major Christian festivals. They love the church in all its wonderful variety and they know that no one style or shape will fit everyone. Over the years, they have had the privilege of working with congregations within all sorts of traditions. They have no desire to change these traditions; what they have done is help worshippers see how much more connected worship can be to the whole of life. I have seen them in action and it was brilliant to watch people not only be inspired as they worshipped, but begin to see how the whole of life can be brought together before the God of the whole of life.

Worshippers come in all shapes, all sizes and from all walks of life: the retired-busy crowd, the worried-well crowd, the living-life-to-the-full crowd, the uncertain-in-faith crowd, the confident-disciples crowd, the juggling-work-and-family crowd. Regardless of whether the service is printed or projected, quiet or noisy, frantic or serene, as we gather we can gain a bigger perspective on who God is and why our lives matter to his ongoing eternal purposes on earth. And if all that sounds too grandiose, we believe that God's purposes are fulfilled in the most unlikely places: offices and garden centres, shops and banks, family centres and bistros, hospital wards and athletic clubs, colleges and nursing homes. These are our frontline locations.

That's why this book really matters.

For over thirty-five years, the London Institute for Contemporary Christianity (LICC) has been proclaiming from every conceivable rooftop that the way to live fruitful lives is to recognize that our everyday lives, our whole lives, matter to God. It's a great vision for life. But it's one thing to help people see the significance of their frontlines; it's quite another to sustain that vision. For it to stay a fresh reality, we need to have a renewed understanding of the God we worship, of the mission that Jesus leads, and the way that the Spirit empowers us today. That will not come by intellectual persuasion but by deep heart-change as we open up our lives to the eternal God in worship.

Sam and Sara remind us that we come before a God who welcomes his people with joy, who urges us to keep on running the race that has been set out for us in our frontline contexts. They remind us that we come

to Mount Zion, to the city of the living God, the heavenly Jerusalem. You have come to thousands upon thousands of angels in joyful assembly, to the church of the firstborn, whose names are written in heaven . . . Therefore, since we are receiving a kingdom that cannot be shaken, let us be thankful,

and so worship God acceptably with reverence and awe, for
our 'God is a consuming fire.'
(Hebrews 12:22–23, 28–29)

So as you read, our hope is that you will be inspired and
equipped to lead the people of God in their worship together,
knowing that in just a few hours they will scatter again to love
and serve the God who first loved them.

Neil Hudson
Imagine Director
LICC

PREFACE

In the past fifteen years we have worked for local churches in rural and urban settings; both full time and part time; as worship coordinators and pastors. We have also served in churches as volunteers, attempting to run worship teams in moments outside our full-time jobs. So when someone comes along with a new 'great idea', the latest viral video, or the most recent book about worship, we will probably join you in rolling our eyes. *Another* idea we have to try and fit in? Our brains were already groaning with things to think about!

Whole Life Worship is not another fad or crackpot theory. It is a passionate call to allow God to expand our view of worship: to take a step back and be amazed by the scope of God's engagement with us, his love for the world he made, and his plans for our lives. It is an invitation to assess church worship less by style and preference or how it made us feel, and more by how it revealed God, who it formed us to be and how it empowers us to be disciples of Jesus in our daily lives.

Beyond our local church, we also have a decade's worth of experience in itinerant ministry across the UK. Through engageworship.org we have been creating resources, training teams, and leading worship for churches, conferences and networks. As this has progressed, there is one theme that seems to resonate most strongly: gathered worship which helps the members of congregations engage with God's heart for the world they live in. As we have dug deeper into this, we have seen people caught up in passionate prayer for their workplaces, schools and streets. We have seen songs that mention God's heart for our world ignite congregational singing. We have given space for honesty about the realities of life and seen broken people encounter the God who cares. We have created resources which help families and individuals connect their everyday lives with God's purposes. This book is about sharing some of this journey and experience with you.

The third thing we have been involved with is studying and teaching worship at the London School of Theology. This has helped us delve into the firm biblical foundation for worship which engages with people's everyday lives. It has also helped us to explore worship from different traditions, times and places, giving us an appreciation for how other parts of the Christian church have engaged their congregations in whole-life worship.

How to read this book

This book is made up of two parts. The first part unpacks the opportunity that planners and leaders of gathered worship have: to engage congregation members with the heart of God for their whole lives. We look at the biblical foundation for whole-life worship (chapter 2) and why gathered worship is so important (chapter 3). We explore a framework for fully rounded, three-dimensional gathered worship (chapter 4) and discuss how the regular journeys of our services can shape a congregation (chapter 5). In the final chapter of part 1 we look at how specific songs strengthen or undermine a 'whole-life' view of worship and discipleship (chapter 6).

Part 2 goes on to unpack a very practical approach to applying this teaching within a local church. It steps through various stages of a worship journey, highlighting how each can include an element of looking outwards to everyday life. Each chapter gives numerous examples of songs, prayers, creative ideas and other worship activities that can be used and adapted for your context.

The book is designed to be read sequentially. A foundational understanding of why and how you might develop your gathered worship will ensure lasting change within your church culture. Resist the temptation to skip straight to part 2, and give yourself time to think through the implications of part 1 for your context.

We have attempted to draw from a wide range of styles in our examples and recommended resources. Whatever stream of the church you come from, we welcome you on this journey. However, you will probably notice that we have come from evangelical and charismatic backgrounds. This worship tradition is one we love and are committed to, but because it is our 'home ground' it is also the stream we critique the most in this book. We pray that God will take us all deeper into what biblical, authentic and world-changing worship looks like, wherever and however we express it.

ACKNOWLEDGMENTS

This book was commissioned by the London Institute for Contemporary Christianity (LICC), alongside the accompanying *Whole Life Worship: Journey Pack* (see <www.licc.org.uk/wholelifeworship>). We are so grateful to the team there for their support, encouragement, critique and passion. In particular, we want to show our appreciation to Neil Hudson, David Leeds, Mark Greene, Tracy Cotterell and Antony Billington. Further thanks goes to the LICC Partners who helped to fund this project.

On 22 February 2016, we held a Consultation Day at LICC with around forty experts in congregational worship from all over the UK. It was attended by pastors, theologians, youth workers, worship leaders, songwriters and industry representatives. They gave feedback on an early draft of the book, explored the wider themes from their perspectives and helped us to shape the whole project. We are hugely grateful for their input. Thanks to (among others) Paul Pease, Jo Vickery, Anita Dobson, Tim Lau, Michael Bolt, Sue Rinaldi, Mark Earey (who also gave significant subsequent email feedback),

Jacqueline Dow, Jacob Arnold, Jeremy Perigo, Anne Harrison, Janet Gaukroger, Ben Forber, Gordy Munday, Stefan McNally, Amy-Jane Wilson, Lou van der Linden, Andy Piercy, David Snelling, Judith Stephenson, Tom Lewis, Andy Stinson, Ben Dear, Charles Hippsley, Michael Bolley, Keith Woolgar, Andrew Belfield, Luke Waldock and Jonathan Robinson.

At early stages of research, we enjoyed Skype conversations with Graham Kendrick, the Revd Graham Cray and Keith Getty. These discussions also contributed much-needed insight, correctives and ideas. Interaction with Sam's colleagues in the Music and Worship Department of the London School of Theology, and with Joel Payne at the songwriting group RESOUNDworship.org, have also made a significant impact on our thinking.

The team at IVP/SPCK have been excellent in all areas of editing and design. Thanks specifically to Steve Mitchell, Mollie Barker, Rima Devereaux, Louise Clairmonte and Mark Read.

We are enormously grateful for our employers, the team of Trustees from the Music and Worship Foundation (MWF), who released us to take a year in Sweden to write the bulk of this book. They have continued to feed into the project through suggestions and encouragement, and their support (along with those who give financially to MWF) makes our work with engageworship.org possible. So 'thank you' to Roger Peach, Ron Jones, Eils Osgood, Timo Scharnowski, Damian Herbert, Lorraine Crook, John Leach and Andrew Mitchell.

Ultimately this book is dedicated to all the local churches, small groups and missional communities with whom we have had the pleasure to minister over the years. They have taught us to value the great variety of worship that springs from faithful congregations, praising God wherever they find themselves. Our prayer is that this book will continue to resource you on this journey of whole-life worship.

Part I

FOUNDATIONS AND FRAMEWORKS

1. WORSHIP AND THE FRONTLINE

> Worship is all-consuming, because God is
> all-deserving. So, we live our lives eager to breathe
> every breath, think every thought, and do every
> deed for the glory of God.
>
> Matt Redman[1]

Andy's story

Andy runs his own business and prides himself on his good work ethic. He is also a Christian and active in leading worship at his church. However, the link between work and worship used to go something like this in his head: 'Through my work I can make money in order to support those who are in "full-time Christian ministry". My work has no inherent value, except for how much money I can make and give away.'

We met Andy when we were leading worship at a Christian conference. A defining moment for him happened during the song 'I Will Worship'.[2] Instead of its typical place at the beginning of the service, we led it at the end of the meeting. Images behind the song words pictured different work situations, and the challenge was to consider how aspects of 'ordinary' life could be lifted up as worship. This was a light-bulb moment for Andy, as he caught his first glimpse of how his whole life could be an offering to God.

Since then he has been on a fascinating journey, grappling with the relationship between worship and life outside church. This has had two exciting consequences: first, Andy now has a renewed enthusiasm for the company he runs; he and his employees have a new purpose and have produced a mission statement that reflects the inherent value that Andy sees in their work. Second, when he leads worship in his church, he now tries to bridge the gap between Sunday and Monday, helping his church move along the same journey he has been on. He says: 'I love it when corporate worship on a Sunday has a relevance to my working week and that church is not an escapist experience. I don't leave my burdens at the church door; I bring them in with me.'

He also ended up using the 'I Will Worship' idea in his own church. He asked people to send in photographs of their work to be used as background images.

> We had a kitchen, a desk, a hand fixing a hinge on to a gate post, a tapestry and more. After the meeting I received a lovely email from one of the contributors saying how much that had helped her view the importance of what she does. Quite a defining moment for her too![3]

Healing the split

At the heart of this book is the conviction that church worship plays a decisive role in transforming congregations into whole-life disciples. There is the potential that each person can be refreshed, inspired, empowered and sent out to make a difference wherever he or she happens to be; that our songs, services and sacraments can proclaim God's heart for the renewal of creation, and infuse each person with a sense of his or her role in God's plan.

The problem is that so much of our gathered worship is currently disengaged from the lives and everyday ministries of the congregation members. As one pastor put it:

> we began to realise that there was a disconnect between what was happening in the building on a Sunday and what was happening in people's lives during the week. It was as though once we left the building, the really important business was over.[4]

Sunday services suffer from a problem affecting many other areas of church life – what has been called the 'sacred–secular divide'. This is an unnatural split or 'dualism', which acts as if the Christian life was split into different segments. Some of these segments are presumed to be important to God, while others are seen as less 'spiritual', somehow further down God's priority list.

This divide is seen clearly in much of our gathered worship. Worship leader Graham Kendrick once challenged the London Institute for Contemporary Christianity to analyse the themes and theology of contemporary hymns and songs, under the question: 'Are we perpetuating an abstract spirituality?' Mark Greene concluded:

> Broadly speaking, the answer to his question was 'Yes'.
> You certainly won't find many songs that express the kind of gritty engagement with daily life that you find in David's psalms, with his frequent references to the tools of his trade, his sense of God's intervention in his daily life as a soldier, songwriter, husband, adulterer, fugitive, father, general, king . . .[5]

This matters because we are formed by what we sing. Songs stick in our heads – recognized in the fourth century by Basil the Great when he suggested that people do not leave church reciting the sermon, 'but they do sing the texts of the Psalms at home and circulate them in the marketplace'.[6] And song lyrics do not merely stay in our heads, but journey down to our hearts and core beliefs. As R. W. Dale put it in the 1800s: 'Let me write the hymns of a church and I care not who writes the theology.'[7]

The issue is not limited to song lyrics. It reaches wider into how we pray, the ways we introduce worship activities, and the kinds of images we use in church. It goes wider still, to the content of the regular patterns and journeys we take congregations on. Most fundamentally it relates to our foundational understanding of what worship is: our theology, our biblical assumptions about what God intends from our worship.

When God's world bumps you on the head

A few years ago, we were leading the youth venue at a national conference, with the typical blend of bright lights, loud music and caffeine-fuelled Christian fun. Sara led a section of prayer for God's world, holding up an inflatable globe as a symbol. As she closed the prayer time, the band began to play an upbeat worship song. We bopped the globe out into the crowd, inviting the teenagers to pray for a part of the world when they caught it. Most of the teenagers got into the spirit of the activity, bouncing the globe around as the song continued, and we soon moved on to another section of the service.

We were surprised, then, to receive a couple of feedback notes at the end of the evening: 'Please do not throw *inflatables* out into the congregation during worship. I found it *most* distracting.' These were unexpected comments from some otherwise relaxed teenagers.

The story of this distracting inflatable world became a parable to us. Maybe we should be open to God's world bumping us on the head every once in a while? To remind us of his heart for the whole world and our whole lives. Perhaps we *need* to be distracted sometimes – not from God, but from our preoccupation with ourselves and a purely inward experience. Or do we continue to pass on to the next generation the idea that 'worship' means 'Close your eyes, raise your hands, sing loudly, and whatever you do don't let yourself be distracted'?

The problem with continuing in this divided, disconnected direction is that our church worship is shaping Christians to think that God is not interested in their everyday lives. Bishop Graham Cray, theologian and former team leader of Fresh Expressions, puts it this way:

> If spirituality is undermined by dualism each act of worship
> can have serious negative consequences on the spiritual life
> of a congregation. Worship becomes spiritualised and
> ethereal, rather than being rooted in daily experience and
> circumstances.[8]

If you are a pastor, or a leader of worship, you will very likely be concerned that your congregation focuses on God. Our lives, and particularly our gathered worship, must be all about God. Amen! But are we revealing and responding to the full picture of who God is, who his people are, and his plans for the whole of creation? Or does our church worship culture paint him and his purposes too narrowly?

Local church story

'A lot of our parishioners are business people who work in the city, so they are quite distant when they come back to our little village. There is the attitude that we leave our problems at the church door and escape reality. So when we sing our songs there is a sense of "I love you, God, but I would rather not talk about that problem in my week, or how I had this really scary business meeting, or how I had to fire someone."'

Amy, worship and youth leader, Church of England

The frontline culture shift

For the sake of God's kingdom and its impact on his broken world, we need a new perspective across every aspect of church life. Neil Hudson describes this as 'a new culture that changes the way we relate to one another; a culture where our activities help us see the potential for everyday mission; a culture that enables us all to become mature, whole-life followers of Jesus'.[9]

Each congregation member is called by God to be fruitful in whatever place he or she happens to be during the week – on his or her 'frontline'.[10] Most of us can only realistically be involved in a church-based activity for up to ten hours per week. There are another 110 hours of the week where we are called (and perhaps best placed) to be fruitful for God's kingdom. There are places where we ordinarily spend significant time with people who do not know Jesus. It might be our workplace, among family members we care for, a shop we regularly visit or a social group we are part of. Can you imagine the impact the church would have if every congregation member was inspired and sent out to be fruitful *there*?

Our language, habits and priorities at each level of our church life need this change of perspective. What is required is not a superficial tweak or momentary fad, but a deep culture shift. Gathered worship has no less of a part to play in this process. Imagine if our songs, prayers and actions on a Sunday reflected God's heart for our everyday lives, for our broken world, for his kingdom come and his will being done:

at the supermarket,
and on the bus,
and in our kitchens,
and in the factory,
and on the playground,
and at the bowls club,
. . . as it is in heaven?

What if our gathered worship inspired and commissioned us out to our 'scattered' existence? What if we were sent out to worship God through the seemingly 'ordinary' things that we do, provided we did them with his strength, in his ways and for his glory?

Local church story
'People cannot always pinpoint a specific moment when God changed something in them, but if we are consistently trying to make the connection within gathered worship to life every day, I think that is like a healthy diet for people. Over time it builds a discipleship that is whole life and continues on into the Monday-to-Saturday life.'
Janet, worship leader, Baptist Church

Non-stop soul shaping

The contemporary church often puts a lot of focus on how our worship expresses emotions to God – our love for him, our need of him, our response to him. This is vital, and we love being part of this kind of worship. But it is possible to forget that as well as expressing emotions our worship is also forming us from the inside out.

Congregation members are powerfully shaped by the worship they engage in, week in and week out. Worship scholar John Witvliet writes:

> In both intentional and unintentional ways, the church is engaged in nonstop soul shaping. This may happen . . . through preaching, sacraments, music, and art . . . Because church life is all about God and God's ways with us, *everything* we do in church shapes how participants imagine God and God's ways with us.[11]

An image that Witvliet has used to describe gathered worship is that of food, forming and nourishing our bodies.[12] We know that if we only put burgers, chips and coke into our bodies, they are going to be shaped in a certain direction! It may not happen overnight, but as a regular 'diet' certain foods will change the way our bodies are formed, with positive or negative results.

When it comes to our spiritual diet, our songs, prayers and patterns of worship form us from the inside out. They shape us at subtle, subconscious and significant levels. Over months and years of feeding on repeated journeys of worship, we are shaped to make particular assumptions about God, ourselves, the world around us, and how these things are all supposed to interact.

Witvliet points towards studies which have found that the attitudes of congregation members towards issues such as the environment, gender roles, race, ethnicity and political attitudes are shaped most significantly by 'seemingly insignificant messages' they receive from regular public worship.[13] A separate 2014 survey conducted across a diverse range of congregations in the UK found that gathered worship was the most significant factor for people's growth in discipleship.[14] The report noted, however, that 'Many of us, worshippers and worship leaders, probably do not think of worship as being deliberately formative.'[15]

How might the attitudes of congregation members be shaped by these small acts, regularly committed or omitted?

- If the congregation is welcomed each week with an encouragement to 'leave your problems at the door', what will we start to believe about God's concern for our everyday lives?
- If global tragedies or disasters are rarely mentioned in worship services, what will we learn about God's attitude towards injustice, or our calling to cry out for the broken?
- If intercessory prayers are only ever for our church's members, or our particular country, what do we begin to believe about God's heart for every nation?
- If the only people asked to come to the front to be commissioned in prayer are those going on overseas mission trips, what do we come to believe about the value of each person's frontline mission?
- If testimonies and song lyrics are only ever from the perspective of people who have everything sorted out, how do those in the congregation come to view their own struggles?

- If creation is only sung and spoken about in idealized terms, what do worshippers pick up about God's attitude towards our misuse of the environment, and our calling to steward it?
- If we never confess sin, or only ask forgiveness for inward, personal sins, what does this imply about the scope of Jesus' salvation and sanctification?
- If the images used as a backdrop for the worship songs are only ever of countryside sunsets and mountains, never of cities, business or anything modern, what is the cumulative impact of these visual cues over many months and years?

These questions should cause us to think carefully, not merely about the songs and prayers we choose, but about the patterns of our worship from week to week. What we include on a regular basis, the shape of our services, and the things we habitually include or neglect have a powerful impact in shaping the attitudes and convictions of our congregations. This is the content of part 2 of this book, where we will walk through different parts of the worship service, and see how these can be approached in ways that will help your congregation members worship with their whole lives.[16] We will also suggest many resources – songs, prayers, creative ideas and activities – which might help you explore these journeys.

However, before we can think about our patterns and resources, we first need to address our underlying assumptions about what worship is. We need to turn to the Bible to see what God intends our worship to be, and how it embraces both what we do in church and what goes on outside those doors. This is where we turn in chapter 2.

2. ALL OF LIFE CAN BE WORSHIP

> Worship . . . must be the one, grand, royal action
> of our whole life, in all our thoughts, words,
> and deeds. We are always God's priests,
> called to serve his holy purposes.
>
> Abraham Kuyper[1]

Whole-life worship

For Christians, all of life can be a response of worship to God
– you have probably heard this before in sermons or books.
Mark Greene writes: 'We live to glorify God. And God is
glorified as his character, his priorities, his goodness and
indeed his power are expressed through our everyday lives.'[2]
Or as Rick Warren puts it in *The Purpose-Driven Life*: 'Worship
is not a *part* of your life; it *is* your life.'[3]

This idea has become almost a cliché when discussing
issues of worship with Christians today. At some point in a
conversation about worship, somebody will pipe up and say,
'Of course, worship is not just about singing songs in church
– our whole lives can be worship to God.' And everyone nods
sagely. Yet when we actually *gather* to worship in church we
do not always demonstrate this truth. Our practice often
gives the impression that the only (or at least main) place and

time we can worship God is when we come to a church service.

The fact that in the evangelical/charismatic church we often refer to times of singing as 'times of worship', song leaders as 'worship leaders' and buildings as 'worship centres' does not help. Or in other traditions, we might think of the priest as the worship leader, and particular prayers and rituals as the full extent of our worship. As important as these things might be, they do not represent the complete picture of Christian worship as revealed to us in the Bible. Biblical scholar David Peterson declares that 'Worship in the New Testament is a comprehensive category describing the *Christian's total existence*'.[4]

Local church story

'Something we are trying to change at the moment is that God is interested in all of your life, not just your songs. People are stuck on the idea that "I can't worship God because I'm not good at singing in tune", whereas it is what you do in your coffee shop, what you do in your workplace that can also be worship to God.'
Jacob, worship leader, Baptist Church

Worship in the Bible

The life, death and resurrection of Jesus Christ fulfils and expands upon the pattern of worship revealed by God in the Old Testament. Jesus completes what this system of temple, priest and sacrifice was intended for. Then, remarkably, he enables us by the Holy Spirit to be his temple, to serve as his priests and to offer our own sacrifices of worship. Let us unpack the implications of each of these points.

Temple

In the Old Covenant, worshippers came to the specific place of the tabernacle (Exodus 25 – 31) or temple (1 Kings 8). This was a particular space in which God was present with his people. God provided a way for his people to come to him through sacrifices, and protected them from his consuming glory by a curtain within the 'holy of holies'. The New Testament reveals Jesus as the fulfilment of all that the temple was meant to be (John 2:19–22). David Peterson explains: 'The temple . . . was both the meeting-place of heaven and earth and the place of sacrifice for purification from sin. Thus, it found fulfilment in the incarnation and the sacrifice of Christ.'[5]

At Jesus' death the curtain in the temple is torn in two (Luke 23:45). This reveals Christ himself as our 'new and living way' to come into the presence of God (Hebrews 10:20). Christian worship is no longer restricted to a specific place, and we can be confident that we can 'draw near' (10:22) into God's presence wherever we are.

Astonishingly, we ourselves are called temples of the Holy Spirit (1 Corinthians 6:19–20). We are a dwelling place for God, bringing him glory at all times, wherever we find ourselves. As theologian Miroslav Volf puts it:

> There is no space in which worship should not take place, no time when it should not occur, and no activity through which it should not happen. All dimensions of human life are the 'temples' in which Christians should honour their God . . .[6]

Priest

The key 'worship leader' of the Old Testament was the high priest; he alone could go into the holy of holies as the representative of the people of God once every year (Leviticus 16).[7] In the New Testament, it is revealed that Jesus is our 'great high priest' (Hebrews 4:14–16). We no longer rely on another human being to make worship possible – Christ is the one true mediator between God and humanity (1 Timothy 2:5), dealing with our sins for ever and leading us into the presence of God (Hebrews 7:23–28).

Because of what Jesus has done for us, every Christian has the privilege of being called a priest, serving him wherever we find ourselves (1 Peter 2:5, 9; Revelation 5:10). One of the words from the Greek Old Testament for the worship offered by priests is *latreuein*. This can be translated as both 'worship' and 'to serve'.[8] This word is used in the New Testament of Anna worshipping in the temple day and night (Luke 2:37), but it is also the term Paul uses in Romans 12:1 as an encouragement to offer our whole selves in worship.[9]

Sacrifice

The giving of animals and other produce was central to the Old Testament worship system, primarily as God's gracious way of dealing with Israel's sin. Even in the Old Covenant, God was concerned not just with going through the motions of the offering. He was interested in the heart and life of the person making the sacrifice – think of Micah 6:6–8 or Amos 5:21–24. As the biblical scholar F. F. Bruce comments:

> In the New Testament and Old Testament alike it is insisted that our relation to God embraces and controls the whole of life, and not only those occasions which are sometimes described as 'religious' in a narrow sense of the word.[10]

But the most radical change comes when Jesus offers himself as the perfect, final sacrifice for our sin (Romans 3:25; Hebrews 10:14).

•

In the light of this, there is nothing we can do to work or sacrifice our way into God's presence – he has done it all. No amount of singing, praying, giving or serving makes us worthy. We come to God by his grace alone. The worship sacrifice we are called to make is not to earn our salvation, but instead is a grateful response *to* our salvation. In the light of the gospel of grace (see the whole argument in Romans 1 – 11), Paul urges us to respond with a *living sacrifice*:

> Therefore, I urge you, brothers and sisters, in view of God's mercy, to offer *your bodies as a living sacrifice*, holy and pleasing to God – this is your true and proper worship.
> (Romans 12:1, emphasis ours)

By 'bodies' Paul is referring to the whole self, as Calvin put it: 'not only our skin and bones, but the totality of which we are composed'.[11] Eugene Peterson expresses it as 'your everyday, ordinary life – your sleeping, eating, going-to-work, and walking-around life' (Romans 12:1, MSG). The response of worship we offer back to God includes every aspect of our existence.

Sacrifices of lips and hands

Hebrews 13:15–16
Similarly, the book of Hebrews sums up the Christian response of worship like this:

> Through Jesus, therefore, let us continually offer to God a *sacrifice of praise* – the *fruit of lips* that openly profess his name. And do not forget to *do good and to share with others*, for with such sacrifices God is pleased.
> (Hebrews 13:15–16, emphasis ours)

The writer describes our response of worship, our 'sacrifice', as being of two related kinds. The first is a 'sacrifice of praise' which the author defines as the 'fruit of our lips': our prayers, songs, testimonies and creeds. They are the audible overflow of our hearts' commitment and thanks to God. What we sing, say and confess verbally can be a heartfelt offering of worship to the glory of God.

But there is also a second kind of 'sacrifice', which is less about words and more about actions. 'Do good and . . . share with others' or as *The Message* version puts it:

> Make sure you don't take things for granted and go
> slack in working for the common good; share what
> you have with others. God takes particular pleasure
> in acts of worship – a different kind of 'sacrifice' –
> that take place in kitchen and workplace and on the
> streets.
> (Hebrews 13:15–16, MSG)

For this New Testament writer, there is a response of worship which comes not just from our lips but also from our hands. It involves our response to God not only within the church congregation, but also among the people we bump into in various situations from Monday to Saturday. It is not merely related to abstract, 'spiritual' matters but to the very practical stuff of sharing our money, food and resources. God can be glorified with these offerings of worship as well.

Colossians 3:16–17

A further passage from the New Testament which underlines this is Colossians 3:16–17. The first verse is often quoted when people talk about matters of worship:

Let the message of Christ dwell among you richly as you
teach and admonish one another with all wisdom through
psalms, hymns, and songs from the Spirit, singing to God
with gratitude in your hearts.
(Colossians 3:16)

This is a rich sentence, explaining how we can let the truth
of Jesus live in us and share it with one another through the
singing of different kinds of songs to God.[12] It is clearly
related to gatherings of worship where people sang together,
and should be an encouragement if you love to sing in
church.

However, Paul's thinking does not stop there, for in the
very next verse he goes on: 'And *whatever you do*, whether in
word or deed, do it all in the name of the Lord Jesus, giving
thanks to God the Father through him' (3:17, emphasis ours).

'Whatever you do', whether it is in word or in action, can
be done as an expression of gratitude to God.[13] Bible com-
mentator Ralph Martin says of this verse: 'there is a sense in
which every phase of life is an act of worship and all our
activities, even the more mundane and routine, can be offered
up as part of the "living sacrifice" we are called to make.'[14]

Paul is expanding the actions of worship beyond singing
and prayer to include potentially *anything* we might do or say.
We can, when we do so 'through Christ', turn every moment,
every task, every conversation and every thought into an
expression of worship.

Local church story
'In my previous church there wasn't this secular–spiritual
divide, and I miss that. I worked as a physiotherapist, and
I felt that they honoured that . . . I suppose I would use the

word "vocation". I was doing it to be Christ's person in my
work, and I was prayed in to that.'
Jacqueline, lay reader, Church of England

Gathered and scattered worship

A core conviction at the heart of this book is that the contemporary Western church has separated worship into two
categories – what we will call:

- *gathered worship*: the worship in specific times and
  places, like Sunday church services, home groups and
  conferences; and
- *scattered worship*: the worship outside church meetings,
  on people's everyday frontlines.

Gathered worship is very important to us! In the next chapter
we will be exploring how and why this aspect of worship is
indispensable to the Christian life. The issue, however, is that
this area of worship is too often separated from the equally
important scattered worship of the congregation, outside
church meetings. Our patterns and prayers, our services and
songs often seem to exist in a little bubble as if they were the
only really important part of worship. They rarely engage
with the issues and perspectives of the congregation members
in their weekday lives.

The problems related to this split include the following:

- Church worship can be experienced as an escape
  from reality. Isolation from the world outside has
  been identified by the Barna research group as
  one reason why young people are leaving churches.[15]

- Congregations can be formed with a skewed picture of God's heart for the world, and his purposes for members' lives.
- Gathered worship can give the impression that it is more important to love God with your heart and soul, while downgrading the equally vital aspects of mind and strength.
- Churches miss the opportunities to bring the weekly triumphs and tragedies – local and global – before God in prayer, lament and thanksgiving.
- Congregation members are not being inspired and equipped to worship and serve God in their week, in their work, leisure and home lives, wherever they find themselves.

It is our longing to help churches hold both gathered and scattered worship as equally vital. To allow our worship in church to draw from our experiences of glorifying God on our frontlines. And for our gathered worship to inspire and equip us to be sent out for richer, more fruitful scattered lives of praise. In this way we can reintegrate the two and embrace the full biblical picture of worshipping God.

3. DOES GATHERED WORSHIP MATTER?

> If members of this community are to remain
> distinctive in an alien environment, they need to be
> gathered as well as dispersed. Community-building
> practices and processes are essential. So too is
> corporate worship, in which the community
> rehearses the biblical story, rekindles its vision
> of a renewed creation and prays for the
> coming of God's kingdom.
>
> Stuart Murray[1]

Should we stay or should we go?

If it is true that every Christian is a temple of the Holy Spirit, a priest of God, and that everywhere can be a place to bring God a sacrifice of praise, then we might ask: does gathered worship matter? Should we focus primarily on the scatted worship of our frontlines? Is there a biblical precedent for meeting together in specific places and times with other Christians, or is this secondary at best?

Similar questions have been asked from a more practical perspective. Given the falling church attendance in the UK and beyond, can we afford to spend our time on meetings? Should we not prioritize going out in evangelism, social action, political engagement or other forms of outreach? Gerard Kelly writes about the contemporary temptation to prioritize either joining together in 'services' or sending out in 'mission':

> It seems that we are being asked to choose between inward focus and outward flow, between gathering and dispersal. This feels dangerously close to asking a dying patient if he would prefer to breathe in or breathe out. We can and must do both.[2]

Is the inhale more important than the exhale? Is the right wing of an aeroplane more vital than the left one? No. Our gathered and scattered worship need to be dependent on each other, inspiring and informing one another in a virtuous circle (see Figure 3.1).[3]

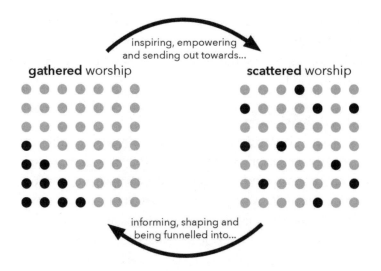

Figure 3.1: The virtuous circle of Whole Life Worship

Abraham Kuyper (1837–1920) was a journalist, pastor, theologian and eventually Prime Minister of the Netherlands. He had a remarkably integrated vision for what the Christian life entailed, and is famous for the striking quote: 'There is not a square-inch in the whole domain of our existence over which Christ, who is sovereign over all, does not cry "Mine!"'[4] And yet Kuyper saw the church service as a unique and pivotal moment in the Christian life:

> It is not, of course, that the practicing of worship consists exclusively in going to church. Rather, it must be the one, grand, royal action of our whole life, in all our thoughts, words, and deeds. We are always God's priests, called to serve his holy purposes . . . However, the service of God for the congregation does not come to full expression until the congregation assembles in worship for the express purpose of bringing God honour, praise and prayers.[5]

For Kuyper, all of life was potentially worship, and yet this was brought into focus and given shape by the practice of gathering as sisters and brothers for obedient, passionate praise to God.

Local church story

'We come back from our lives on our frontlines to share some of the encouragements and be healed from the hurts – that's what we do in our gathered worship. But that is not an end in itself, so we go back out to the frontline, in order to take Jesus with us. We get this from Isaiah 2, where the people say, "Come, let us go up to the temple of the Lord, for there the law of the Lord goes out." They have a whole worship experience in that gathered worship, but the last verse says, "Come, O Israel, let us walk in the light of the Lord": they go back out to carry God's light.'
Paul, church leader, Free Evangelical

Early church gatherings

We can see this kind of dynamic in the early church. We have already explored the holistic view of the New Testament, where every aspect of life was to be offered back to God as a sacrifice. But we can also see that the first believers do continue meeting together for specific times and in specific places. The people of Israel practised daily times of prayer (Psalm 55:17; 119:62, 164) and it seems that this was inherited by New Testament Christians. We read of them meeting together at these scheduled opportunities, both at the temple and, increasingly as the church moved away from Jerusalem, in private homes (Acts 3:1; 10:9).

Beyond this, they also began to emphasize Sunday – the first day of the week or 'the Lord's Day' – as their key time to gather together and break bread (Acts 20:7). One of the earliest sources we have describing early Christian worship outside the Bible is a document called the *Didache* (late first century or early second), which encourages its readers: 'on every Lord's Day – his special day – come together and break bread and give thanks.'[6]

Why gather?

Why did the early Christians make gathered worship a priority? Why is it important for us today? We want to suggest three reasons for this. In gathered worship we:

- are reminded that we are different;
- remember the story;
- receive God's empowering.

Reminded that we are different
In the previous chapter we mentioned 1 Corinthians 6:19, where individuals are described as temples of the Holy Spirit.

But Paul also uses this image corporately, of the whole church: 'God's temple is sacred, and *you together* are that temple' (1 Corinthians 3:17, emphasis ours; see also Ephesians 2:21–22). David Peterson comments on this passage:

> The people of God continue to be the Spirit-filled community when they disperse and go about their daily affairs, but their identity as 'the temple of the Lord' finds particular expression when they gather together in Jesus' name, to experience his presence and power in their midst.[7]

So our first point is this: gathering together as believers is vital because here we are reminded who we are – a sacred temple; the set-apart people of God.

Jesus prays for his disciples that they may be sent out into the world, but are not to be 'of' the world. Instead they are to be sanctified by the word of God (John 17:14–16). Gathered worship is a specific opportunity to be reminded that although we are engaging with the world, we are not to have the world's values.

Paul encourages us not to conform to the pattern of the world, but be 'transformed by the renewing of your mind' (Romans 12:2). Peter describes us as 'a chosen people, a royal priesthood, a holy nation, God's special possession'. Gathered worship is a place to become secure and sure in that identity, so that we might be sent out to 'declare the praises of him who called you out of darkness into his wonderful light' (1 Peter 2:9).

Local church story
'One of the things we do is use "secular" music in acts of worship. We made a video using the song "Fix You" by

Coldplay, and set that alongside images of Jesus being crucified. It meant that when people left the church and heard the song again on radio or on the TV, the images which we had offered to them came into their heads. It helped to translate the worship they had been part of, out of the church and into their lives.'
Andy, vicar, Church of England

Remembering the story

Second, it is important to notice that the first Christians broke bread together when they gathered, listened to preaching (Acts 20:7), and sang songs which helped the word of Christ dwell in them (Colossians 3:16). They were reminded not simply of who they were, but of the bigger story of what God had done, was doing and would do in the future.

We hear all kinds of competing stories when out in our scattered lives – stories which focus around selfish ambition, faithless worry and godless striving. The symbols, words and sounds of gathered worship give us an opportunity to refocus on the radically alternative story of God: the God of self-sacrifice, who cares about the whole earth, and sends us out to play our part in his re-creation. Eugene Peterson writes:

Worship is the time and place that we assign for deliberate attentiveness to God – not because he is confined to time and place, but because our self-importance is so insidiously relentless that if we don't deliberately interrupt ourselves regularly, we have no chance of attending to him at all at other times and in other places.[8]

Gathering to read Scripture, tell stories, engage in communion and sing songs together allows us to relocate ourselves and our lives in the bigger story of God. And as we find ourselves in that story, it begins to form our ways of thinking and acting differently. As Graham Cray puts it:

> One of the vital things about church gathered – in all its forms – is actually about the reinforcing and the supporting of habits that help you live consistently when you are not with Christians. You've got to be a little bit careful, that in addressing the dangers of turning church into a holy huddle, you don't undermine its importance as a character-forming community.[9]

Receiving God's empowering

Third, gathered worship creates space to be refreshed by God's empowering Spirit. It is not that this is impossible when we are scattered. Yet there is a sense that gathering together helps us focus and receive in ways which we may struggle to replicate out on our frontlines. When we gather we are reminded that all of our worship, gathered and scattered, is totally reliant on God to make it possible. As Volf puts it:

> worship is something human beings owe God . . . but our arms are lifeless and our mouths dumb if God does not give them strength and facility of speech. We can give God only what we have first received from God.[10]

We see this happening to the believers in Acts 4, where shortly after Peter and John had been released from prison they went back to the gathered church to pray and worship. The result is that they were filled with the Holy Spirit and received boldness to go out and proclaim the gospel (4:31). Gathered worship can provide a context where we can be refilled by God and sent out.

The writer to the Hebrews encourages his readers to pursue gathered worship – 'not giving up meeting together, as some are in the habit of doing' (Hebrews 10:25). The purpose of such meetings was not simply to have an inward, individual experience of God, but 'encouraging one another', and to 'spur one another on towards love and good deeds' (10:24).

If you are involved in planning and leading worship, be encouraged that God has given you a high calling. Our gatherings are vital for the glory of God, for the building up of his people and for the transformation of the world around us. Let us be inspired and equipped by God to craft services that engage in these three dimensions.

4. IS YOUR WORSHIP 3D?

Our corporate worship serves God,
one another and the world.

Mark Earey[1]

Three-dimensional worship

Both gathered and scattered worship are vitally important if
we are to live a whole life of devotion and service to God. As
planners and leaders of gathered worship, the challenge we
face is how to relate and integrate these two areas. What tools
will help us shape and evaluate our preparation and leading
of gathered times? And how can we emphasize the importance of frontline worship without losing other vital features
of gathered worship? We want to suggest that you ask: is my
church's worship 3D?

Don't worry, when we say 3D we are not asking you to
upgrade your projection screen and hand out funny glasses
to the congregation. By 'three dimensional' we are referring
to language developed by missional church pioneers to unpack
the three essential dimensions of church (see Figure 4.1).
Every church needs the 'Up' dimension (worship to God), the

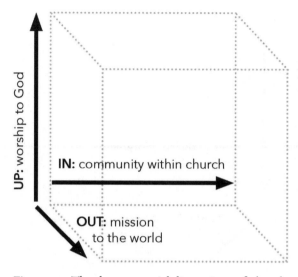

Figure 4.1: The three essential dimensions of church

'In' (community relationships within the church) and the 'Out' (missionary calling to the world).[2]

A development of this idea is to say that *every* aspect of church life needs, in different proportions, to contain each of these dimensions. Church worship is usually filed in the 'Up' section of this model, but we want to suggest you consider how gathered worship can *itself* be 3D. When we gather to worship God we may begin with the 'Up' dimension, but we also need to include the 'In' and 'Out' dimensions.

The 'Up/In/Out' language can sound a bit one-directional. So we are going to say that worship needs to include a 'vertical' dimension (up and down, between God and us), a 'horizontal' dimension (side to side, between one another in church) and a 'third dimension' (being informed by, and sent out to, the situations beyond the church's doors). Or, using more relational language, worship needs to include our relationship with God, one another, and the world beyond our services (see Figure 4.2, overleaf).[3]

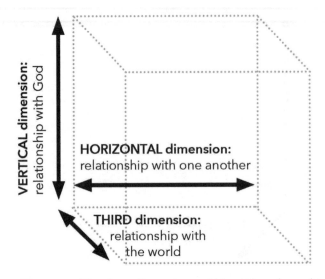

Figure 4.2: The three dimensions within gathered worship

How could you use this model to assess your church's gathered worship?

'Vertical' gathered worship

Gathered worship which takes into account the vertical dynamic is the most common and, arguably, the most important. There is a danger when talking about worship in relation to the church's mission, our frontlines or other such topics that our gatherings become primarily about something other than God. Worship can become an instrument, a means by which we achieve something else. For some churches this is evangelism; for others it is to motivate volunteers for social action; for others still it might be education, or the transmission of information, or the emotional well-being of the congregation. All of these things are important, and ought to be present in our meetings. But we must make sure that our priority in meeting is first and foremost to seek *God* together

– to hear from God and respond to God; to receive from God and to be sent out by God.

Revelation and response

One way to speak about the importance of this dynamic is with the language of 'revelation' and 'response' – what Ralph Martin calls the 'two-beat rhythm' of worship.[4] Many times in the Bible we see characters having a fresh revelation of God's character or activity, which then spills over into heartfelt response. Think, for example, of the Israelites' response in music and dancing at the revelation of God saving them from the Egyptian army (Exodus 15:1–21), or Mary's song of praise at hearing that God would bring salvation through her son (Luke 1:46–55), or Peter kneeling in awe at the revelation of Jesus' power (Luke 5:8–10).

Perhaps one of the issues we have with contemporary worship is that we have got very good at the 'response' part – songs and prayers that say 'I love you, Lord', 'I feel you close', 'I will give my life' – but we have left out the 'revelation' part. So Christians turn up on a Sunday morning with their heads full of other things, and the worship leader wonders why the people are not responding. What should they be responding *to*? In part 2 we will be giving lots of practical ideas about how to ensure a balance between revelation and response.

Local church story

'For us there is quite a tension between our gathered worship and our everyday lives. A lot of the songs we sing have quite a narrow focus – just "I" or "me" and focusing only on "Jesus died for me".'

Kathryn, vocal coach and worship leader, Free Church

'Horizontal' gathered worship

The second dimension reminds us that another unique part of gathered worship is that we come to God *together*. Paul writes: 'Let the message of Christ dwell among you richly as you teach and admonish *one another* with all wisdom through psalms, hymns, and songs from the Spirit' (Colossians 3:16, emphasis ours).

Notice two of our dynamics in this verse: we sing 'to God', but we also sing to 'one another'. Our resources should operate on the horizontal as well as vertical dimension. When Paul is criticizing the Corinthian church members for their disorderly and selfish worship, he reminds them: 'When you come together, each of you has a hymn, or a word of instruction, a revelation, a tongue or an interpretation. Everything must be done *so that the church may be built up*' (1 Corinthians 14:26, emphasis ours). Worship resources should involve a variety of people, and should help us build one another up.

We live in a very individualized society. This has spilled into our church worship, where many of the songs are written as 'I' rather than 'we'; our activities often involve closing our eyes or staring over someone's shoulder at the stage; and it is rare that we are encouraged to interact with the person next to us. Including the horizontal in worship goes against the dualistic split we spoke of earlier, because worship cannot be purely about an inward experience if you are reminded of your brothers and sisters around you. Truly communal worship offers opportunities to share the joys and sorrows of living on our frontlines, to open our eyes to the needs around us and to be more fully 'present'.

As people experienced in the ups and downs of worship leading, we understand completely the fears which horizontal, participatory worship evokes in a pastor or worship leader.

There is a genuine worry that if we open up the meeting for contributions from the congregation we will get one of two responses:

1. Complete silence reigns as nobody engages, or . . .
2. Someone says something that is pastorally inappropriate, theologically inaccurate or just plain embarrassing!

These are very real fears. You are correct to be concerned by them. This is why we have spent some time thinking about ways in which our resources can encourage horizontal involvement while also retaining a degree of pastoral safety and security for the congregation. What follows are two example resources to illustrate how this horizontal worship can work. There are many more 'ideas to try' to be found in part 2 of this book.

Ideas to try: 'Psalms Praise'

Ask people to open their Bibles at the book of Psalms, then sing a simple, celebratory song. After you have sung it for a few minutes, bring the volume down and invite people to read a verse or a sentence from a psalm that jumps out to them (stress that they are not to read a whole psalm). You can keep the music or rhythm going on underneath, but make sure people can be heard. In a bigger group you might need to pass a radio mic around. We have used this lots of times now, and it helps people who would never pray out loud to speak up. The members of the congregation begin to play their own part in leading and shaping each other's praise. Quoting directly from the Bible ensures a degree of theological and pastoral safety.[5] If you are concerned that it might take some people to 'get the ball rolling', then prepare a few congregation members to be the first to join in.

Ideas to try: 'He's My Saviour' song[6]

This is a simple song which encourages horizontal involvement. You can sing the four verses, which proclaim the ancient truth 'Christ has died, Christ is risen, Christ will come again'. But you can then invite people in the congregation to share a word or phrase they would want to sing to Jesus. The leader can then fit this into the song: 'He's the King of kings'; 'My provider'; 'How I love him'. Again, we have used this countless times – in small groups, regular-sized churches and large youth venues where we have had to use a couple of radio mics. As with Psalms Praise, you often get the sense that some of the things being shared are very timely and sometimes costly; for example, the person who says 'He's my healer' when he or she has yet to see God's healing in a personal way, or says prophetically and with faith 'He's my Prince of Peace' in the midst of struggle.

'Third dimension' gathered worship

Our third dimension – relating to the world beyond the church doors – is probably the most challenging of the three. Connecting gathered worship with people's everyday scattered lives has always been a struggle for the church, and choosing or creating resources which do this in effective and engaging ways can be a tough task.

However, imagine the benefits when congregations are connected on a Sunday with the God who cares for the world, who is sending and equipping Christians for their frontlines, and whose mission will renew the whole of creation. Like your first experience of a 3D image or film, connecting congregations on all three dimensions will bring gathered worship to life, making it 'pop' out of complacency and spread into every sphere of people's experience.

We would define a 'third dimension' worship resource as something which intentionally engages a congregation with God's heart for a sphere outside the church doors. That could include work, education, social issues, family life, justice causes, politics, environmental concerns, community building, and more. The question to ask of your resources is: do any of the songs, prayers or activities we use intentionally focus our congregation outward, and help our people face the issues out on their frontlines? Below are two songs which illustrate this 'third dimension' approach; again, you will find more such ideas in part 2.

Local church story

'I felt quite inadequate and frightened when I first considered ministry on my frontline, trying to live and serve in that place, but I felt God saying, "Don't worry, I am already there with them." I put that into a song and shared it in a service. A man who was about to move house to a new job working with the homeless told me that this was really helpful for him, that he heard God promise to be with him too.'

Anita, discipleship and families worker, Church of England

Ideas to try: 'Lord, You Hear the Cry' song

This song by Geraldine Latty is a very effective way to turn people's attention to God's heart for situations outside the church walls:

> Lord, you hear the cry
> of the widow weeping;
> Lord, you hear the cry
> of the child ill-treated;
> Lord, you hear the cry
> of the depressed one sinking . . .[7]

After each verse and chorus we respond to God using that simple, ancient prayer *Kyrie Eleison*: 'Lord, have mercy.' The song mentions situations that we do not normally sing of in worship: the proud ones laughing; the childless hoping; those in debt and struggling; even the addict craving.

Its scope is both personal and global: God hears 'the greed of nations', and his justice will 'roar in mighty waves across the earth'. It also mixes both honest lament and passionate, biblical hope in God: 'Lord, we hear the sound of your kingdom coming; Resurrection Day for creation groaning.' And the final words show the commitment of the singers to be part of God's solution: 'Mercy I receive, pouring out in loving.' It is musically accessible and engaging, and we have used it in many different contexts. This is the kind of song which ought to be part of the regular repertoire of any church wanting to inspire the congregation towards whole-life worship.

Ideas to try: 'Christ Be in My Waking' song

This song names different periods and spheres of life – waking, working, resting, sleeping. It is ideal for reminding the members of the congregation that they can and should be worshipping God out on their frontlines, with the chorus:

> Jesus, this is my devotion:
> All my life to know You,
> Every day to walk with You.
> Saviour, You're my deepest longing,
> You're the One I live for,
> Teach me, Lord, to walk with You.[8]

Stuart Townend has written about what he was intending with this song on his blog:

We seem to have lots of songs that focus on the experience of worshipping – 'Here I am Lord in Your presence' type songs. So in recent years I've tried to create songs that will be relevant to the other 6 days and 22 hours of our week! . . . It's a reminder to be 'God-aware' in all the different parts of our lives – from morning to evening and night, in my thought-life, in the things I say, in the good things . . . and in our most desperate moments.[9]

We find the honesty of this song very effective, particularly in the final verse: 'Christ when hope has faded, nothing left to cling to, every pleasure jaded, every well is dry.' When was the last time you sang a line like that in church? This is another song which deserves to be part of your regular diet.

We will be giving lots more specifically third-dimension resource ideas in part 2. However, in order to reshape gathered worship to engage better with our whole lives, we need to do more than simply change the words of our songs and prayers. This shift requires that we rethink our patterns of worship, the journeys we take congregations on each week.

5. NEW JOURNEYS OF WORSHIP

We possess integrity because we have crafted
our worship experiences to be a continuation
of the challenges of our lives, rather than
an escape from it.

Andy Flannagan[1]

What are your patterns?

As we begin to consider whether our gathered worship is 3D,
it is important to look not only at individual songs and prayers
but also at the wider patterns we use, week by week. Do our
repeated journeys of worship help the congregation members
engage with God, one another, and the world beyond the
church?

At this point, some of you may be saying, 'But I don't have
repeated patterns in my church', or even 'Repeating a service
structure is the enemy of life-giving worship!' Both of us grew
up in Baptist-type congregations, 'free' churches, where the
assumption was that we had left the constraints of traditional
worship behind. 'Liturgy', from our perspective, was reading
the same words out of a book every week. It seemed very
boring, dry and the exact opposite of the freedom we were
looking for.

However, as we began to experience gathered worship in other churches, we realized that there was more to this than we had assumed. We learned that the word 'liturgy' comes from a Greek word which also gets translated 'worship'. *Leitourgein* is used over a hundred times in the Greek Old Testament to refer to serving God or ministering in the tabernacle or temple.[2] It is used in the New Testament in similar ways, but also for what the New Testament church was doing when the believers came together for worship (Acts 13:2). Many consider the roots of the word to be 'the work of the people' or 'the people's work' – so 'liturgy' is basically the things people do when they gather together to worship God.[3]

Every church has patterns of worship – a form of liturgy. These might be written down, carefully discussed or imposed by a denomination. They could equally be unspoken, rarely questioned and invented by the local church. But they are still patterns, habits, regular journeys. Often, when we go to a new church to lead worship, we ask, 'What is your usual order of service?' and the church leaders reply, 'Oh, we're very informal! There is little set structure.' So we will plan a service and then on the morning when we arrive the pastor will say, 'Oh, but we always have a welcome at this point', or 'We need to take the offering after that bit', or 'The children have to leave then', or even 'We don't do things like that in our worship!'

Every church, in this sense, is 'liturgical'. The real question is: are the repeated service patterns we follow on a regular basis helping to shape us with the full picture of who God is, how he sees us, and his perspective on our calling to his world?

Local church story
'I was in church and they were singing the calling of Isaiah 6 to be a prophet to the nations: "Who will go for us?" In that

moment I had that sense of my life being for something
beyond coming into corporate worship; that the Christian
life is about making God known in relationships, whether
that is in my neighbourhood or the nations around the
world. I really had that sense of corporate worship colliding
with mission and God's heart for the world in that moment.'
Jeremy, theology lecturer and worship leader, Assemblies of God

Patterns through church history

As Christian worship has developed over the centuries, certain
patterns have arisen. One very common order involves
'gathering', hearing God's 'word', responding at the 'table'
(the Lord's Supper) and finally engaging in a 'sending'.
Constance Cherry calls these the four 'rooms' of the traditional worship service, and she notes different things which
can often happen within each room.[4] These might include the
elements shown in Figure 5.1.[5]

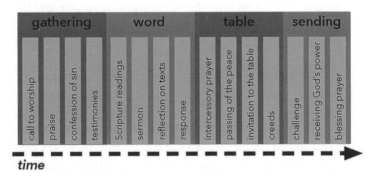

Figure 5.1: The four 'rooms' of the traditional worship service

It may be that this kind of shape is very familiar to you or
that it looks quite different from what you are used to. A
pattern like this *can* help to emphasize different sides of God's

character. The various aspects of worship can take the congregation on a journey towards recognizing private and corporate sin (in confession); catching God's heart when praying for the world (in intercession); or acknowledging God as Creator of the heavens and the earth (in a creed). And ultimately the direction of the service can aim towards the sending, where people are empowered and commissioned to go out to love and serve the Lord in their everyday lives.

We say *can* because it is quite possible to follow this kind of shape to the letter, and yet miss out on all of its outward-looking, whole-life implications. The service planner and leader of worship needs to have his or her eyes open to the potential inherent in this kind of shape.

But it is also true that other shapes of worship have emerged in more recent years. These shapes have their own in-built priorities and shaping potential.

Contemporary/charismatic patterns of worship

The nineteenth-century frontier revival meetings in the USA pioneered new shapes of gathered worship. In order to reach unbelievers, the revivalists dropped a more structured 'liturgical' worship style. Instead, an extended time of singing served as a warm-up to the preaching, and they closed the service with an altar call (see Figure 5.2, overleaf).[6]

Everything in this journey serves the preacher's message. It is not difficult to see that this shape has been adopted by many evangelical churches, with Bible teaching for believers replacing the evangelistic message. Ralph Martin notes that a similar shape was also adopted by liberal churches, but here the gospel message was replaced by a call to social action.[7] In all these models, the journey of worship leads to teaching and some sort of response.

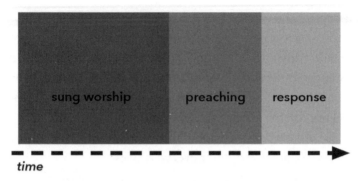

Figure 5.2: Contemporary 'revival' service pattern

Within charismatic circles, the emphasis has shifted to the first section. Often the 'sung worship time' has become, in many contexts, 'the worship', and the goal of this time is an intimate encounter with God's presence as we sing. John Wimber of the Vineyard Church popularized a five-phase model. This has been interpreted as a flow of songs which move through: 1) invitation, 2) engagement, building to 3) exaltation, 4) adoration, and then getting quieter and more personal towards the ultimate goal of 5) intimacy – that is, encountering the presence of God individually (see Figure 5.3).[8]

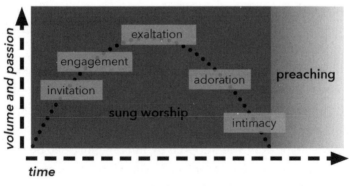

Figure 5.3: Vineyard Church five-phase model of
charismatic worship

Have you ever wondered why, so often, a contemporary worship 'set' will start with loud songs and progress steadily towards quieter songs? This is a direct result of how people have interpreted Wimber's model – or unknowingly inherited a version of it.

Now, this pattern can be very useful. We have used versions of it ourselves, and are aware that many people have encountered God both in conversion and in a fresh renewal of his presence when it has been employed. The issue, however, is whether as a regular diet it is *enough*. If these are the only patterns we use, then it is possible that the congregation is only being shaped in one particular direction.

If the goal of 'intimacy' only implies quiet, uninterrupted individual encounter, there is the temptation to avoid anything 'distracting'. The music remains soft, the words of the songs vaguely about God's love. Practices like reflecting on Scripture, confessing sin, praying for the world, joining in the Lord's Prayer (all ancient patterns which helped congregations focus beyond the church walls) are removed or sidelined, and there is often no space for other art forms apart from music. When the goal is 'intimacy' in this narrow sense, other parts of worship (and especially the ones which relate to our frontlines) take a back seat.

What if our goal every week was not just that narrow definition of 'intimacy'? What if, in meeting with God and hearing his heart, we had the sense of his passion for justice? Or his concern for our everyday problems? Or his joy over someone fulfilling his or her calling at work, school or in the home? This would require different patterns for our worship, which complement and expand our picture of God and one another, and how he is calling us to engage with his world.

Issues of style

It is important to note that we are not asking you to switch denominations or change the personality of your church's worship. Each church's style reflects a different but equally valid aspect of approaching God.[9] The varied journeys of worship across the Christian church have different aims in mind, and each can teach us something about loving God with all our heart, soul, mind and strength (see Table 5.1).[10]

Table 5.1: Various Christian worship traditions viewed as aspects of Mark 12:30

Aspect of Mark 12:30	Intended result	Streams that emphasize this	In gathered worship this can look like
Heart	Concrete decisions	Methodist/ Baptist/ Evangelical	Preaching, altar calls, activism, word-based hymns
Soul	Powerful feelings	Pentecostal/ Charismatic	Singing, prayer ministry, gifts of the Spirit, spontaneity
Mind	Clear understanding	Lutheran/ Reformed/ Bible Church	Word-based hymns, preaching, liturgy
Strength	Specific actions	Orthodox/ Catholic/ Anglican	Eucharist, baptism, processing, crossing self

There is nothing to say that one tradition is necessarily more 'outward-looking' than any other. We need to celebrate the strengths of our own style, but also learn from the other approaches in order to have a rounded picture. We are not recommending that you radically shift your emphasis next Sunday – this would confuse and alienate the majority who connect with your usual services. The trick is to be faithful and sensitive to your 'default style', and yet at the same time be open to incorporating aspects of worship which you can learn from other traditions.

Ideas to try: prayer within sung worship

For example, a church could be committed to a style of singing contemporary-sounding songs in a flow of worship. The members could also be convicted that they ought to be praying for the world as a regular pattern within their services. In chapter 10 we describe how you can incorporate intercessory prayer in the midst of singing. Your songs could lead from praise into a reminder of God's care for the whole world. Then images of the item being prayed for could be projected as the music continues instrumentally, and the worship leader could encourage the people to lift their voices for the situation, or sing an appropriate chorus or refrain as a kind of sung intercession (see Figure 5.4). The time could conclude with a prayer or song trusting in God's power to change the situation.

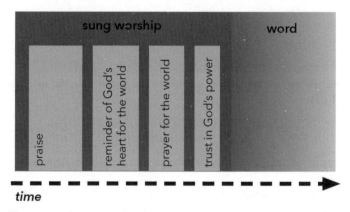

Figure 5.4: Incorporating intercessory prayer into sung worship

Ideas to try: clipboard prayers

As a contrasting example, a church might love its structured, traditional communion service. The members of the congregation might also develop a sense that they are not hearing the stories of their joys and struggles from their frontlines. We once went to a church where helpers passed out clipboards and pens as the service began, inviting people to write down items for prayer or praise from their week, and then collected these in with the offering plate. Later on, a service leader included these small testimonies and requests as part of a time of intercession. Tea-light candles were also made available on a table, so that individuals could go and light a candle when their prayer request was being read out. The hymn following the prayers then went on to highlight God's care for each person. It was a beautiful, pastoral and stylistically appropriate way to incorporate people's daily lives within the journey of worship (see Figure 5.5).

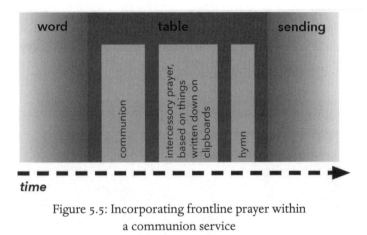

Figure 5.5: Incorporating frontline prayer within
a communion service

Before you move on, take a moment to consider what journeys or shape of worship you regularly take your congregation on.

Are there aspects that intentionally help people look outwards towards their daily lives? Hold these thoughts in mind, as we will explore them further in part 2.

6. THE LANGUAGE OF SONGS

Music in worship is not only about personal
encounter with God. It is about an encounter
which sustains and equips us to receive and
release the power of the Kingdom into
our circumstances and society.

Graham Cray[1]

Lyrics and real life

Nick Page wrote an irreverent but challenging book called
*And Now Let's Move into a Time of Nonsense: Why Worship Songs
Are Failing the Church.* In it he points out that he could find
virtually no 'modern' images in worship songs, 'an image, that
say, could only have come from the twentieth century'.[2]
Instead, we use a kind of Christianized code language, where
we speak of concepts like money and finance using archaic
terms like 'silver and gold', or sing about shepherds and fields
while standing in an inner-city church.

This lyrical escapism can create a barrier between people's
everyday experiences and their encounters with God in church
gatherings. Worship becomes detached from normal life as it
is lived. In contrast, Page argues that 'worship has to be real.
It has to reflect and draw on the reality that surrounds us. It
has to be connected to real life, because worship is real life.'[3]

Songwriter and record-label manager Sue Rinaldi puts it this way:

> Sometimes we [songwriters] are in a church bubble where we don't understand people's everyday experiences or what they would like to listen to. It is a challenge to find language that relates to people in our songs, and to make it sound credible. But we can learn from other genres that do this: street rap, country and western, and so on. These writers have found ways to talk about everyday life, using metaphors that are current, and we can take heart from that. This is a challenge, but one that we must accept.[4]

It is true that it remains difficult to include contemporary imagery in songs without the lyrics losing poetry, becoming 'clunky' or seeming childish. And yet the problem goes deeper. Mere cosmetic tinkering with a few song lyrics will not be enough to transform gathered worship. In previous chapters we saw the vital need to enrich our theological perspectives and to explore different patterns of worship to fuel fully 3D services.

We are strong believers in gathered worship being expressed in a whole host of different ways, using a variety of art forms. Nonetheless, singing remains one of the key ways congregations are able to express unified praise to God, and we therefore want to spend some time considering the lyrics we ask people to sing. Beyond Page's challenge to use phrases and imagery that connect with everyday life, there is also a deeper question of whether the language of our songs reinforces the sacred–secular divide. This is an unbiblical split between gathered worship and life outside church, which leads worshippers away from God's concern for the whole of their lives.

Duelling with dualism

This dualism which sees some aspects of life as 'sacred' and others as 'secular' (and therefore unimportant) has its roots in Greek philosophy. Since its earliest times, Christianity has struggled to shake off the influence of Plato (472–348 BC). This philosopher saw physical things and bodies as evil. For him only spiritual, immaterial things were good and eternal. The neo-Platonic worldview entered parts of Christianity through those we now call the Gnostics. They embraced the dualism of soul and body, material and spiritual, and emphasized spiritual, hidden 'knowledge' over physical existence. Theologian Tom Wright argues that throughout church history and up to today many people suppose that the neo-Platonic position is what Christians believe. This has had a marked impact on the words of our songs. As Wright puts it:

> A good many Christian hymns and poems wander off unthinkingly in the direction of gnosticism . . . [In this flawed view] the created world is at best an irrelevance, at worst a dark, evil, gloomy place, and we immortal souls, who existed originally in a different sphere, are looking forward to returning to it as soon as we're allowed to.[5]

Whether you are choosing songs for a congregation or attempting to write them yourself, it is very important that you consider whether the song lyrics imply a dualistic worldview or emphasize the biblical picture of God's heart for all of his creation. The outlook of a congregation is powerfully shaped by unknowingly singing dualistic lyrics. As Graham Cray writes: 'worship is where above all we proclaim our priorities, and are formed by the Spirit through what we proclaim, and perhaps especially by what we sing.'[6]

We are going to explore four biblical themes, core doctrines that oppose this dualistic worldview: creation and fall; incarnation; cross and resurrection; and our eternal hope. Then we will consider briefly how these themes are reflected or obscured by popular worship songs today. To do this we analysed the top twenty-five Christian Copyright Licensing International (CCLI) songs in the UK and also the top twenty-five from the USA at the time of writing.[7]

1. Creation and fall

In contrast to the creation myths of other religions, the Bible proclaims that all of creation – physical and spiritual – is created by God. The very opening line of the Bible proclaims: 'In the beginning God created the *heavens* and the *earth*' (Genesis 1:1, emphasis ours). There is no sense here that what God really intended was mainly a spiritual life, and that the physical nature of our bodies and the world was a mistake. He looks at the things he has made and he calls them good. Theologian Christopher Voke states that

> there is no merely secular part of life that is outside God's interest or rule. He created it all, and therefore trouble and joy, life and death, worship and family, field and temple, all belong to God . . . There is no 'secular realm' over which he has no rule.[8]

Paul unpacks this further and shows the role of Jesus in this comprehensive act of creation:

> For in him *all things* were created: things in *heaven* and on *earth*, *visible* and *invisible*, whether thrones or powers or rulers

or authorities; all things have been created through him and
for him.

(Colossians 1:16, emphasis ours)

The fall (Genesis 3) impacts all of these spheres of life. But the
fall was not a problem of our physicality, our human bodies
or our existence in a 'secular' world. The problem in the
biblical worldview is sin: rebellion against God; trusting,
obeying and glorifying something which is not God.[9] Paul
diagnoses the problem of the human race by saying that we
'worshipped and served created things rather than the Creator'
(Romans 1:25). This false worship is called idolatry. This can
mean literally bowing down to a statue, but it more often
means 'bowing down' in our hearts towards created things
(Ezekiel 14:3; Colossians 3:5).

Creation and fall in song lyrics
It is notable that out of all the songs we looked at, only three
speak about God as the Creator. One is a traditional hymn,[10]
and another is a setting of the Apostles' Creed.[11] So in fact,
only one of the original contemporary worship songs reflects
the idea that it was God who created the earth: 'You stood
before creation, eternity in your hand, you spoke the earth
into motion.'[12] This scarcity suggests that we need to be
writing and searching out more songs which make explicit
God's good creation of all things, in heaven and on earth. In
this way people might begin to see the world as an integrated
whole, through biblical eyes.

There are a few songs in our sample which refer to the earth
positively. The second verse of the hymn 'Great Is Thy
Faithfulness' proclaims that all the seasons, the sun, stars and
all nature give witness to God's love and faithfulness (from
Psalm 19),[13] while the modern 'Revelation Song' expresses the

idea that we join creation in singing praise to God (from Revelation 4:11).[14]

However, most of the other songs reflect the trend noticed by Pete Ward when he analysed worship songbooks from the 1980s. The world outside church is spoken of as a dark, troubled place. In the language of many worship songs the only place where people expect to encounter God is when we come to church and sing.[15] The full extent of God's presence is limited to when people gather and look to heaven.[16] In the songs we analysed, there was virtually no language of expectation that the believer will worship, serve or experience God in the world outside the church.

There is also no mention of our call to steward the earth, of the fall's impact on creation or concern for the way that we have treated the environment. Christopher Voke comments: 'Creation is not to be seen merely in terms of wonder, thankfulness and joy. Its abuse by humankind and the decay to which it is subjected are to be reasons for penitence and serious consideration in public worship.'[17]

A good example of a hymn lyric (outside our sample of fifty) which attempts to take these themes of creation stewardship seriously is this one by Fred Pratt Green:

God in such love for us lent us this planet,
Gave it a purpose in time and in space:
Small as a spark from the fire of creation,
Cradle of life and the home of our race.

Thanks be to God for its bounty and beauty,
Life that sustains us in body and mind:
Plenty for all, if we learn how to share it,
Riches undreamed of to fathom and find.

Long have our human wars ruined its harvest;
Long has earth bowed to the terror of force;
Long have we wasted what others have need of,
Poisoned the fountain of life at its source.

Earth is the Lord's: it is ours to enjoy it,
Ours, as God's stewards, to farm and defend.
From its pollution, misuse, and destruction,
Good Lord deliver us, world without end![18]

2. Incarnation

A second thread of biblical teaching which cuts against a dualistic worldview is that of Jesus Christ coming as a fully human person. John 1 proclaims that the eternal 'Word of God', the one who spoke creation into being, 'became flesh and made his dwelling among us' (John 1:14). In the early years of the church many battles were fought to hold on to the fact that Jesus was both fully God, but that he also somehow 'emptied Himself' (Philippians 2:7, NASB) and became fully human. He came to a specific time and place, as a physical person, and lived the perfect human life by the power of the Holy Spirit.

Attempts by early heretics to show that Jesus was not 'really' human, more of a Superman masquerading as Clark Kent, were shown to have dire consequences for the gospel. Instead, the church in its creeds affirmed the Gospel accounts where Jesus was born physically from a woman (Luke 2:7), was genuinely hungry (Matthew 4:2), thirsty (John 19:28), tired (John 4:6), and suffered physical pain on the cross (Mark 15:34). Jesus was 'one of us' and therefore understands our human suffering and temptation. As the writer to the Hebrews says of him: 'we do not have a high priest who is unable to feel sympathy for our weaknesses, but we have one who has

been tempted in every way, just as we are – yet he did not sin'
(Hebrews 4:15).

Local church story

'We ran the multisensory "Experience Easter" journey at our
church. One small girl engaged with a station about how
Jesus had felt lonely in Gethsemane. She really identified with
that – there were difficulties in her family, and she had often
felt lonely herself. Her whole understanding of that loneliness
was quite significantly changed because she realized Jesus was
with her in that loneliness. It is a very powerful way of
worshipping, when all the senses are involved like that.'
Joe, vicar, Church of England

Incarnation in song lyrics

There are five songs in our sample which mention Jesus
becoming human as a baby.[19] In particular, 'Here I Am to
Worship' and 'The Servant King' are commendable for their
focus on Jesus coming in humility, poverty and service.

These two songs, however, are noticeable exceptions in
highlighting the human life of Jesus. The vast majority of our
contemporary songs make little or no reference to the bulk
of the Gospel narratives. This has not always been the case;
Pete Ward says of the 1960s songbook *Youth Praise*:

References to the earthly life of Christ fill almost every page.
From the lyrics it would be possible to construct in some detail
the events recorded in the Gospels. The songs dwell at length
on the life of Jesus, from his humility and birth, his miracles,
and his ministry, to the story of his Passion, death and
resurrection . . . while affirming the lordship of Christ,
[*Youth Praise*] never loses sight of the humanity of Jesus.[20]

These kinds of lyrics fade away as contemporary worship develops through the twentieth century and up to today. How many resources do you use that reflect Jesus' earthly life? When have you ever sung of his temptations, his struggles, his rejection, his engagement with different kinds of people, his selfless service, his obedience and so on? The result is that congregations are not being fed a diet of biblical truth about how Jesus demonstrated and made it possible for us to live ordinary, everyday human lives for God's glory.

A song that offers something of a model for how we could move forward with this is the very popular 'Oceans'.[21] When you look at the lyrics it seems that we are being placed in the position of Peter, during the 'walking on water' story from Matthew 14:22–33. There is a good degree of honesty being drawn from Peter's position – he is in the unknown, and his feet may fail. The song embraces the idea that it is only as Peter steps into uncertain waters that he finds the grace and security of being in Jesus. By reflecting on a Gospel story from the life of Jesus we are able to imagine taking steps of faith today (the song is not explicit about this, but the connection can easily be made) as we step out of church and into God's will for us on our frontlines. There are a few other models of songs based on stories from Jesus' life (outside our sample of fifty), such as Graham Kendrick's 'All the Room Was Hushed and Still'[22] or 'The Summons (Will You Come and Follow Me)' by John Bell of the Iona Community.[23]

3. Cross and resurrection

This fully human Jesus died a genuine, bodily death on the cross, and he was physically resurrected to new life. In Luke's Gospel, Jesus goes to great lengths after the resurrection to

prove to his disciples that he has not returned as simply a
spiritual being – he eats fish and says to them, 'Look at my
hands and my feet. It is I myself! Touch me and see; a ghost
does not have flesh and bones, as you see I have' (Luke 24:39).
The risen Jesus has a physical human body, although it is transformed and perfected in that it can appear and disappear
(24:31, 36) and ascend to heaven (24:51).

This resurrected body has implications not just for our
spiritual well-being but for our whole selves, and the entirety
of God's creation. In Ephesians, Paul is determined to demonstrate the universal scope of Christ's death and resurrection.
He describes at least three levels on which the cross and
resurrection have power:

- on an individual level, resurrecting us from the death
  of sin and guilt in Christ (Ephesians 2:1–10);
- on a relational level between us as humans, destroying
  the barriers between Jew and Gentile in Christ's body
  on the cross (2:11–18);
- on a cosmic level, the unification of 'all things in heaven
  and on earth under Christ' (1:10).

Scripture does not force us to make a choice between the
salvation of individual souls and the salvation of God's
creation. Every level of what God has made will be redeemed,
sanctified and restored through the death and resurrection of
Christ. As Paul puts it in Colossians 1:19–20 (emphasis ours):
'For God was pleased to have all his fulness dwell in him, and
through him to reconcile to himself *all things*, whether things
on earth or things in heaven, by making peace through his
blood, shed on the cross.' This gives us another clear mandate
to engage with all of the aspects of God's creation, which he
himself has redeemed.

Cross and resurrection in song lyrics

Many of the songs in our sample spoke of the cross, and a number speak of the resurrection, or more generally of Jesus saving from sin or setting us free. However, the scope of the cross and resurrection is almost always limited to the soul of the individual being saved. As one song states: 'You stood before *my* failure, and carried the cross for *my* shame, *my* sin weighed upon your shoulders, *my soul* now to stand.'[24]

Of course, it is biblical (and also emotionally arresting) to consider that Jesus died for *me*, that *my* sin is forgiven and *I* can spend eternity with God. These songs are right to affirm this. It just seems tragic that we barely ever take the next steps we see in the New Testament of acknowledging that the cross has saving power for *all people* and *all of creation*. Although it does not mention the cross specifically, the closest to this we get in the sample of fifty is the chorus of Kendrick's 'Shine Jesus Shine', which speaks of 'the land' being filled with God's glory and 'the nations' being flooded with grace and mercy.[25] Perhaps this universal scope is part of the lasting appeal of this song.

Surely this is an untapped seam for songwriters? What could be more inspiring for a congregation than to know that Jesus' cross and resurrection is the way by which all people can be reconciled, and how his creation will be restored? Because we have the power that raised Christ from the dead working through us (Romans 8:11; Ephesians 1:18–21), we can help to bring that reconciliation and restoration to the world around us now. These are themes we have attempted to express in our song 'Christ Was Raised', which moves from the personal implications of the resurrection, to our partnering with God in renewing creation, to the reconciliation of all peoples:

Christ was raised, even death could not contain him.
We are saved, Satan's power he overcame.
No more shame, no more guilt and condemnation,
in his name, in his name.
Christ is raised, he is seated with the Father,
and the Spirit that raised him gives us life.
So we'll live to the glory of our saviour,
Hallelujah, he's alive.

Christ was raised, the restorer of creation,
by his grace making earth and heaven new.
we are changed, agents of his re-creation
in all we do, all we do.
Christ is raised, so our struggles have a purpose,
he's alive, so our work is not in vain,
and we'll serve for the glory of our saviour,
Hallelujah, Jesus reigns.

Christ was raised, bringing all the world together,
making peace, breaking down our walls of hate.
And one day every knee will bow before him,
for his praise, for his praise.
Christ is raised, with a new and glorious body,
scars of love in his hands and in his side.
So we'll sing to the glory of our saviour:
Hallelujah, King of life.[26]

4. Eternal hope

While it is right to get excited about the breadth of God's plan
for all he has made, we also need to recognize that there is a
tension here. We are waiting for God to fulfil all that he
achieved in the cross and resurrection, when Christ returns.
As Paul describes it:

> For we know that all creation has been groaning as in the pains
> of childbirth right up to the present time. And we believers
> also groan, even though we have the Holy Spirit within us
> as a foretaste of future glory, for we long for our bodies to be
> released from sin and suffering. We, too, wait with eager hope
> for the day when God will give us our full rights as his adopted
> children, including the new bodies he has promised us.
> (Romans 8:22–23, NLT)

Our eternal hope is not merely spiritual in this passage – the
physical stuff of earth is groaning and yearning 'in hope that
the creation itself will be liberated from its bondage to decay
and brought into the freedom and glory of the children of
God' (Romans 8:21). We ourselves are not simply hoping to
be whisked off to a purely spiritual heaven, but are anticipating
'the redemption of our bodies' (8:23). Jesus' transformed,
perfected human body is the 'firstfruits', revealing how the
whole creation, and our own bodies, will be transformed and
perfected (1 Corinthians 15:20–23). Wright comments:

> Paul speaks of the future resurrection . . . as the reason,
> not for sitting back and waiting for it all to happen, but for
> working hard in the present, knowing that nothing done in
> the Lord, in the power of the Spirit, in the present time will
> be wasted in God's future (1 Cor. 15:58).[27]

Eternal hope in song lyrics

Christopher Voke laments that if 'the church is encouraged
to see its destiny entirely in other-worldly terms in heaven,
and if this world and all in it is to be finally destroyed, the
primary task is spiritual preparation for that world'.[28] This
seems to be the view that is furthered in many of our worship
songs.

For example, Melody Green's 'There Is a Redeemer' has an other-worldly approach to eternity: 'When I stand in glory, I will see his face, there I'll serve my King forever, in that holy place.'[29] It places our 'forever' in another place, not the creation God has promised to perfect. Similarly, Tom Wright is critical of the final verse of 'How Great Thou Art', with its language of Christ coming and 'taking me home' to somewhere else, rather than renewing *this* place.[30] The recent adaptation of 'Amazing Grace' by Chris Tomlin includes one of John Newton's less sung verses, with the very dualistic line 'The earth shall soon dissolve like snow'.[31] One blogger has suggested that a more biblical adaptation might be 'The earth shall be redeemed by God'.[32]

To get the full biblical picture, it is important that we are singing lyrics of God's restoration and renewal of all things – heaven and earth, physical and spiritual. It is also vital that we hold the tension that God has begun this renewal, but that it will not be fulfilled until Christ returns. In the meantime, we can work and play our part in welcoming God's kingdom 'on earth as it is in heaven' today. Anything less than this will have us slip into either triumphalism or hopelessness.

We will finish this chapter, and part 1 of this book, with a great example of how a biblical approach to our eternal hope can work in a song. Geraldine Latty's 'On That Day' both looks forward to God's new creation and also asserts the role that God calls us to play now. May it inspire us to write and choose songs that engage congregations with God's full picture for our whole lives.

> On that day there will be no injustice.
> On that day there will be no more poor.
> So today I will love, I will live, I will work,
> I will join in to see your kingdom come.

On that day, there will be no more sickness.
On that day, there will be no more death.
So today I will love, I will live, I will work,
I will join in to see your kingdom come.

Jesus, thank you for the price you paid,
to bring your heaven to today.
At great cost you brought your world into our world:
We live to know your presence now,
to see your kingdom come.[33]

Part 2

PRACTICAL EXAMPLES

INTRODUCTION TO PART 2

Bearing fruit

Imagine for a moment a beautiful, healthy tree. The kind that has deep roots, strong enough branches to hang swings and hammocks from, and whose leaves bring a rich shade on a sunny day. Just as this tree has grown steadily over time, we would love to see your church worship grow in a healthy and organic way. This will lead to your gathered worship bearing fruit – congregations transformed to live entirely for God's glory. This book encourages you to give attention to three key areas of your gathered worship 'tree': roots, branches and leaves (see Figure P2.1, overleaf).

Deep roots
In the first half of this book we looked at our roots, exploring the vital role gathered worship has in forming and empowering whole-life disciples (chapter 1). We laid biblical foundations in chapter 2, showing that Christian worship can be an offering

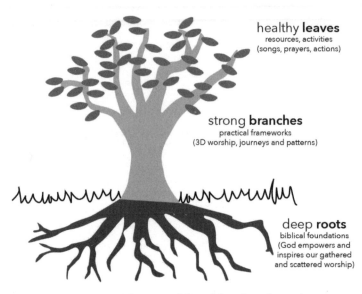

healthy **leaves**
resources, activities
(songs, prayers, actions)

strong **branches**
practical frameworks
(3D worship, journeys and patterns)

deep **roots**
biblical foundations
(God empowers and
inspires our gathered
and scattered worship)

Figure P2.1: The tree of fruitful gathered worship

of our whole lives, including the scattered worship we offer when we are not in church. Yet we established that our times together in services remain essential: for forming Christians who know who they are in Christ, are immersed in his bigger story of the renewal of creation, and are equipped by his Spirit to go out and live for him (chapter 3). These three chapters form strong roots from which the tree of your worship can grow. The rest of the tree cannot be transformed unless you reflect on these foundational ideas first. To begin at any other level will lead only to superficial change.

Strong branches

In chapter 4 we then suggested some strong branches or frameworks that will help us begin to put this into practice. We encouraged you to ask, 'Is my church's worship 3D?' and unpacked the ways in which we can engage congregations in the 'vertical', 'horizontal' and 'third' dimensions of worship.

As you read on, you will find the second half of the book full of further practical ideas for acts of worship that move in these three dimensions, particularly that more difficult 'third dimension'.

We found in chapter 5 that every church has default journeys and styles, which shape us in different ways. Our encouragement remains that you do not try to dismiss your existing style, but instead allow a 'whole life' perspective to be integrated into your current practices. Think of this integration like yeast in dough: although the yeast looks insignificant and small, disappearing into the mix of other ingredients, it lifts the dough and changes its entire structure. And as you find ways to reflect on your current practices, you might find it helpful to learn from other styles and journeys of worship, choosing to include elements from elsewhere appropriately within your own services.

To help you with this, in part 2 of this book you will find different aspects of a church service – some of which will be familiar to you, others of which you may want to consider as additions to your regular journeys. As we discussed in chapter 5, how many of these you include and in what order will depend on your tradition and context. Chapters 7 to 16 draw out how each aspect can relate to the congregation's growth as whole-life disciples, and to their ministries on their frontlines. In other places we have related the aspects to our three dimensions: 'vertical', 'horizontal' and the 'third dimension' out beyond the church walls.

Healthy leaves

Think of the things you do in your gathered worship – your songs, prayers, creative expressions and activities – as leaves on your 'worship tree'. Leaves are integral to a tree and essential to its life, but they also grow and fade regularly. We aim to give you a wide range of examples of worship ideas in part 2. Pay attention to the songs and activities you choose for worship, but also acknowledge that they can – like leaves on a tree – change regularly and differ significantly from church to church.

Some of the ideas we suggest will fit easily within your church's comfort zone, and we hope that some will be immediately usable. However, there will be some ideas that may be unsuitable or more challenging for your congregation. Consider how you could adapt these ideas for your own context. Some might require a different musical arrangement, more or less use of technology, a change of language, or another creative reframing in order to communicate well with your people. You might even take the essence of an idea and express it in a completely different way.

We talked at length in chapter 6 about how song lyrics can reinforce or counter a dualistic mindset towards God's world. The songs we suggest in the rest of this book offer positive examples of lyrics that reinforce the biblical story of God making, redeeming and re-creating the earth, and our role in partnering with him in this kingdom project. Continue to reflect on the kinds of song words you are choosing, so that whether you use our suggestions or not, the musical diet is a biblical one, empowering your congregation for whole-life worship.

Focus on gathered resources

We have intentionally focused on acts of gathered worship, rather than providing devotional activities aimed at people's 'quiet times'. There is great benefit in having specific prayers and other resources to use in our daily lives, but our primary goal here is that the church's gathered worship will feed and shape your scattered worship. We hope that worship practices which the congregation engages with in church (whether that be a song, a reflective prayer idea, or the instinctive cry of 'Let your kingdom come!' or 'Lord, have mercy') will trickle down to our frontlines, and serve as pit-stops and reminders. But we also desire that these resources will point beyond themselves towards the wider task of glorifying God in everyday life. Here we can serve him and bless the world he loves in all our deeds, words and actions.

7. GATHERING

The way the congregation is gathered,
welcomed and called to worship will cast
a certain light over the whole service.

Michael Goheen[1]

Local church story
'People can find it difficult to connect church services
with what happens in life outside. Sometimes they are just
exhausted, and really they are just there to receive and be
built up, so they see coming to worship on Sunday as a
recharging to go out to face another stressful week.'
Judith, vicar, Church of England

Starting right

From the very beginning of a service, planners and leaders of
worship have the opportunity to fully engage the worshippers
who are coming straight from their frontlines. There is little
point in a church having a value of whole-life worship if the
worship leader welcomes people in with words indicating that
the real worship only begins now. Equally, it will be difficult

for the preacher to convince his or her listeners that God is interested in their whole lives if the person gathering the worshippers has asked them to leave their problems at the door.

The first part of the church service is a junction, or a pivot point, between scattered and gathered worship. We may ordinarily focus on the fact that this moment is the beginning of something, but it is equally important to keep in mind that it is also the conclusion of something else: worship on our frontlines.[2] When we, as worship leaders, feel frustrated at a perceived lack of engagement or enthusiasm from the members of our congregation in the beginning of a service, we might need to consider how to meet them where they are.

Constance Cherry likens leading worship to being a host, welcoming guests to your home.[3] From this perspective, starting the service with an emotional response song is like meeting your friends at the door with a deeply personal question. When friends visit your home, you may arrive at the deeply personal question but it will be later, after the initial greeting and conversation. Part of the gathering time is about a caring welcome.

We might also like to think about the opening part of our service in terms of the 3D model we discussed in chapter 4. What are the key ways to engage the vertical, the horizontal and the 'third' dimension in the opening times of a service?

The vertical dimension

Why does the church come together to worship? An outsider visiting might deduce that the worship is centred around the act of singing ('Let's stand to sing' may be the first words uttered in the gathering), or perhaps the practical details are most important ('Could I ask you all to move towards the centre of the pews?'), or perhaps even the amusing details of the pastor's life ('Let me tell you about something funny that happened on the way here . . .'). Instead, right at the beginning of the service we can choose to focus the congregation on God's invitation to draw near to him. As Cherry says: 'It makes a great difference who initiates worship, for God's call transforms church from a meeting of the minds to a meeting with the living God. Worship is not a meeting *about* God; it is a meeting *with* God.'[4] Traditional liturgical greetings, such as 'The Lord be with you / And also with you', are designed to help us acknowledge the presence and need of God as well as the presence of one another.

This does not, incidentally, need to exclude any awareness of our frontlines. This God, who called us first, is also the God who calls all of humanity; who loves and cares for the whole world. Meeting with him is also hearing his heartbeat for the things we encounter in our scattered worship lives. Fanny Crosby's hymn 'To God Be the Glory' expresses this well – we are invited to 'come to the Father through Jesus the Son', so that the whole earth might hear God's voice. Or take a look at 'Come, People of the Risen King',[5] which encourages us to come from every walk of life and every circumstance.

Reading from the Bible as the first words spoken in the gathering is a strong way to emphasize the vertical dimension. John 4:23 might be read, where Jesus states that the Father is seeking true worshippers who will worship in the Spirit and in truth; or perhaps a section of a psalm, such as Psalm 66 ('Shout with joy to God, all the earth!'); or for a tired congregation, a suitable selection might be Jesus' invitation in Matthew 11:28–29 for those who are weary and burdened to come to him.

Ideas to try: 'In the Beginning' prayer
We often use this prayer by Mark Earey at the beginning of
a service together. It focuses us on the Creator God and his
intentions for us in the service. We play atmospheric music
underneath and put the words on the screen with awe-inspiring
photographs taken by the Hubble telescope:

[*Leader*] In the beginning, God created the heavens and the earth.
In the empty void and crushing darkness, God spoke
light into being.

[*All*] **Creator God, bring light into our darkness.**

In the beginning, God took eternity and formed time
and space, seasons, days and years.
Creator God, fill and shape the time you have given us.

In the beginning, God took land and sea and filled them
with life of every kind.
**Creator God, help us find our place within your diverse
creation.**

In the beginning, God spoke his very image,
and the returning echo formed humanity.
**Creator God, open our eyes to see you reflected in
every human face.**

In the beginning, God created,
and it was good.[6]

The horizontal dimension

The first thing visitors to your church see when they enter is
not your carefully worked-out mission statement, or your
creed, or even how sincerely you worship. Before anything

else, you are speaking to your congregation through the physical environment. Clayton Schmit states that 'the most visible things in worship are those that bear the greatest significance for the community'.[7] Are you only able to see other people's necks and the person on the platform or in the pulpit? If possible, can you find a way to change the seating arrangement to look more like a meeting of friends than a concert or lecture which is simply there to be watched? Once the music begins, can everyone hear themselves and their neighbours sing? It can be disheartening for congregation members to realize that whether they sing or not is irrelevant, as any sound they make is covered by the volume of the PA system.

Ideas to try: 'We Are One in Christ' poem

As well as considering our physical and aural environment, we can find prayers and other ways to acknowledge one another in the gathering moment of a service. Using a poem like our 'We Are One in Christ' is one way for everyone to recognize that we are all different, and come from different places, but that we can find unity in Christ:

[*Leader*] We are many,
         God's great diversity,
[*All*]   **yet we are one in Christ.**

         Different faces,
         different races,
         yet we are one in Christ.

         Butchers, bakers,
         website makers,
         bankers, tailors,
         teachers, sailors,
         yet we are one in Christ.

Fathers, mothers,
sisters, brothers,
single, married,
broken, carried,
yet we are one in Christ.

The happy, the clappy,
the barely out of nappies,
the ancient, the modern,
the famous, the forgotten,
yet we are one in Christ.

Some hopeful, some hopeless,
some cope well, some cope less.
Some sure and some doubt,
some whisper, some shout,
yet we are one in Christ.

Those with abundance,
those with need,
those who are generous
or wrestle with greed,
yet we are one in Christ.

Elbows, tummies, knees and noses,
kidneys, femurs, teeth and toeses.
Some unmentionable, some protected,
some accepted, some rejected,
yet we are one in Christ.

A broken body,
torn apart,
mars God's image,
breaks God's heart.
And yet our Father knows how the end will be,

> when all his kids will sing in harmony,
> the bride will dazzle, her branches bloom,
> so add your voice to hymn the tune
> **that we are one in Christ**.[8]

We often add sign language in the response to underline the message and make the poem more interactive, and the repeated words make it helpful in a multigenerational setting. If you like to start your service with singing, Sam's song 'Come You Thankful People' is another helpful way to draw people together and recognize our unity in diversity, with words like:

> Come you thankful people come,
> to praise the one true God;
> come as many, come as one,
> to praise the one true God.
> We've travelled here down many ways,
> to praise the one true God,
> and all of us have parts to play,
> to praise the one true God.[9]

The repeated line in the verses, again, helps to involve those unable to read.

Ideas to try: 'Blessed Be Your Name' introduction

This PowerPoint slide[10] shows four images from Matt and Beth Redman's popular song 'Blessed Be Your Name'.[11] The idea is to get people to reflect on what kind of road they travelled to get to church that day. Was it 'by streams of abundance' or 'walking through wilderness', with the 'sun shining down' on the path, or a 'road marked with suffering'? This resource then becomes more 'horizontal' if you invite those in the congregation to share the road they most relate to (or another image which fits them better) with one or two people around them (see appendix 2 for thoughts on small-group discussion in church). The concluding prayer intentionally welcomes people from all kinds of situations, and encourages them that, whatever 'road' they are on, they have something to bring to worship:

> (We say together:)
> If you're splashing in streams of abundance,
> we welcome you – share your joy.
> If you're parched in a desert wasteland,
> we welcome you – share your doubts.
> If you're relaxing in the light of contentment,
> we welcome you – share your peace.
> If you're stumbling on a road of suffering,
> we welcome you – share your pain.
>
> (We pray together:)
> God of water, earth, light and brokenness,
> we welcome you, as you welcome us.
> Amen.

Local church story

'The way churches often do the notices in the beginning of a service is, in many places, a missed opportunity. Which bits of the human story beyond the church get told in the notices, and which don't? Often we just talk about the church's internal agenda: what's coming up next week, the prayer meeting, the summer fete or whatever it might be. This is the chance to bring in the stories of the congregation members, to find out what's going on in the

wider world. Why don't our notices include more of what
is going on in the wider community, for instance? Why
don't we give opportunities for people to say how their
week has been?'

Mark, theology tutor, Church of England

The third dimension

The vertical and horizontal examples we have so far given in
this chapter already highlight aspects of whole-life discipleship. Yet we can also choose to gather the congregation with
a special focus on the third dimension – connecting directly
with people's lives of scattered worship. We ought to be
proactive about choosing gathering words which recognize
that the week leading up to this moment matters to God. As
Schmit puts it:

> Regardless of how a congregation elects to begin its time of
> adoration, leaders can invite people into the gathering with
> a knowledge that they have come from days of active service
> and worship in the world. As previously they have been sent,
> here they attend to the need for God's people to come
> together again . . .[12]

Ideas to try: 'And I Saw Satan Fall Like Lightning' poem
Bob Hartman wrote a wonderful piece themed around 'the
sending of the seventy-two' in Luke 10, which illustrates
beautifully how we can acknowledge and celebrate what God
has done between the sending and the present gathering:

> After this the Lord appointed seventy-two others and sent
> them on ahead of him, two by two, into every town and place
> where he himself was about to go. And he said to them, 'The

harvest is plentiful, but the labourers are few. Therefore pray earnestly to the Lord of the harvest to send out labourers into his harvest . . . '

The seventy-two returned with joy, saying, 'Lord, we volunteered at the local food bank!'

And he said to them, 'I saw Satan fall like lightning from heaven.'

'And, Lord, we baked cakes to raise money for refugees.'
'And I saw Satan fall like lightning from heaven.'

'And, Lord, we told Bible stories to children in schools.'
'And I saw Satan fall like lightning from heaven.'

'And, Lord, we joined a community gospel choir.'
'And I saw Satan fall like lightning from heaven.'

'And, Lord, we prayed daily for the people on our street.'
'And I saw Satan fall like lightning from heaven.'

'And, Lord, we made a meal for our grieving neighbours.'
'And I saw Satan fall like lightning from heaven.'

'And, Lord, we listened when a workmate talked about her
    failing marriage.'
'And I saw Satan fall like lightning from heaven.'

'And, Lord, we mowed the lawn for the old couple at the end
    of the close.'
'And I saw Satan fall like lightning from heaven.'

'And, Lord, we listened when you spoke and went where you
    sent us, no matter how big or how small the call.'

'And I saw Satan fall like lightning from heaven.'
I saw Satan fall like lightning from heaven.
I saw Satan fall like lightning from heaven.[13]

Ideas to try: 'As We Gather' song

An example of a great contemporary song in this context is 'As We
Gather (Whatever We Do)' by Joel Payne. The verses list things
we might do, in both gathered worship and scattered worship.
After each line we respond 'Lord, we will worship'. The third
verse gets very specific:

> In the course of every working day,
> Lord, we will worship;
> when our business takes us far away,
> Lord we will worship.
> When we care for children in the home,
> Lord we will worship;
> when our audience is you alone,
> Lord we will worship.[14]

The chorus then proclaims:

> And whatever we do, in word or deed,
> we do for the one who sets us free;
> when we're on our feet or on our knees,
> Lord, we will worship.

This song acknowledges the scattered worship we have been
engaging in through the week, and also prepares us for the
gathered worship we are about to share in.

8. PRAISE

True praise is not just an internal Christian affair,
it is witness in and for the world.

J. G. Davies[1]

Glorious praise

Praise is giving God the glory he deserves. It is proclaiming who he is, what he has done and what he will do. It is central to the worship of the Psalms, the New Testament, and the church throughout the ages in its set texts and its spontaneous exclamations. In Revelation 5:11–13, we get the striking picture of every creature in heaven and on earth declaring praise to God the Father and Jesus 'for ever and ever'. And whether it is sung in Vivaldi's 'Gloria', Henry Lyte's 'Praise, My Soul, the King of Heaven',[2] Matt Redman's 'We Welcome You with Praise'[3] or the Caribbean 'Halle, Halle, Hallelujah',[4] congregations across the world love the energy and joy which singing praise to God generates.

Using our 3D terms, it may seem at first glance that this is a mainly 'vertical' act of worship. It is true that, in praise, we receive from God revelation of who he is and what he has done, and then we offer it back to him. In this part of gathered worship, God's character and deeds are particularly focused upon. However, as well as being vertical, congregational praise can be 'horizontal'. In gathered worship we praise God *together*, with 'one mind and one voice' (Romans 15:6). Paul tells us that our attitude towards one another is itself a way to bring glory: 'Accept one another, then, just as Christ accepted you, in order to bring praise to God' (Romans 15:7). By speaking and singing out praise with our brothers and sisters, we encourage one another and remind each other of God's character and acts.

Praise in the third dimension

In addition to the horizontal and vertical dimensions of praise, there is an often-missed 'third dimension' angle, relating out to the world beyond. This can be seen very clearly in Psalm 96:[5]

> Sing to the LORD a new song;
>   sing to the LORD, *all the earth.*
> Sing to the LORD, praise his name;
>   proclaim his salvation day after day.
> *Declare his glory among the nations,*
>   *his marvellous deeds among all peoples.*
> (Psalm 96:1–3, emphasis ours)

Psalms like this reminded Israel that they were not to be like the other nations, falling into idolatry (96:5). On the other hand, Israel was not to hide away from the rest of the world, becoming inward-looking. Instead, the people of God were to proclaim his character and acts to the whole world (96:3).[6] They were blessed by God in order to be a blessing to the nations – an idea also seen in Psalm 67:1–2 (emphasis ours):[7]

> May God be gracious to us and bless us
> and make his face shine on us –
> *so that your ways may be known on earth,*
> *your salvation among all nations.*

As God's people we declare his praises – who he is and what he has done – so that the whole world might know and receive his salvation.

Local church story
'Often when people express appreciation for the worship we have led, the most frequent adjective I hear is "uplifting". Now, nobody wants to be a purveyor of depressing worship, but I sometimes worry that what we are creating is at best a displacement activity, and at worst some form of drug. Once the high is over, does that really fuel you for the rest of life?'
Jonathan, church musician, Church of England

General and specific praise

As we engage in praising God, we will notice two categories beginning to emerge. 'General' praise is completely appropriate and necessary. Rather than focusing on specific reasons, it remembers that God is always worthy of praise. General praise includes phrases like 'Lord, you are good', 'Hallelujah', 'Glory to God' and 'Lifting you higher'. This is vital vocabulary for the people of God, and as congregation members learn to speak and sing it out in church, they can also begin to carry it out on to their frontlines.

However, we also see another category in both the Psalms and historic Christian worship: 'specific' praise. This is when we are reminded of a particular act of God and give him glory for that. John Witvliet writes that

> Large portions of Hebrew prayer are devoted to recounting the history of God's actions (which presumably God already knows!). This act of remembrance does much more than merely tell a story. It gives identity and specificity to the God who is addressed in prayer, and correspondingly, to the people who pray.[8]

In many of the psalms we see testimony that is both personal (116; 118) and corporate (114; 136): how God has saved and delivered in the past. This praise is not general or ethereal – it is rooted in historic events. This gives shape to our praise, and helps to form the congregation as the people of God.

In much contemporary worship this 'specific' praise appears to be missing. Our praise can be disconnected from the actions of God in history, and the actions of God today in the world and on our frontlines. Alan and Eleanor Kreider describe how 'The worshippers may praise God at great length, but without specifically rooting their praise in the story of God's liberating acts and the vision of God's new creation'.[9] In order to remedy this, you could try reading short passages of Scripture that remind people of God's bigger story and acts (see chapter 9 for examples). There are also written liturgical prayers that praise God for his specific acts in history, for example, the ancient *Te Deum*.[10] Or experiment with tying your times of praise in to testimony from the congregation (see chapter 12 for ideas).

Ideas to try: images for 'Praise to the Lord'

Another way to make your praise specific, and highlight the third
dimension, is through the images you use on a projection screen.
Visual media like photographs, videos and illustrations can add
another layer of meaning to a song, a psalm or a prayer.

An example of this is the images we have used behind the
hymn 'Praise to the Lord, the Almighty'.[11] In the first verse we
have used an image of a beautiful, rural landscape. This
emphasizes the 'king of creation' line. However, in verse 2 we
have used an image of the financial district in the City of London.
Can you imagine the way this adds to the meaning of the line
'Praise to the Lord, above all things so mightily reigning'? What
does it mean that God reigns over bankers, corporations and
industry? How will someone who relates to that image interpret
the line 'all you have needed has been met by his gracious
ordaining'?

In the third verse, which speaks of God 'prospering our work',
we have used the image of an ordinary suburban high street. This
helps the congregation praise God for the very specific, everyday
ways in which he helps us with our work. You could use other
images from your local area, or visuals that reflect other aspects
of work, to emphasize how God 'daily attends us' on our frontlines.
For more tips on using digital images well, see appendix 3.

Songs of specific praise

Another way to add a specific and frontline angle to your praise
is within the words you sing. Look out for lyrics that describe
an aspect of the biblical story of God – creation, his engagement with Israel, his coming in Christ, and his eventual plan
to renew heaven and earth. Or choose songs and hymns that
speak of what he is doing in the world today, and aspects of
his character that influence life on our frontlines.

Ideas to try: 'Shout It' song

A great example of this is Geraldine Latty's 'Shout It'.[12] It
encourages the congregation and all of creation to 'shout the
news' – to proclaim or broadcast the glories of God's character.
These include the fantastic truths that 'the silenced voice can
sing again', 'the ones abandoned [are] found again' and 'the
hopeless can believe again'. This is the God who is 'with us – for
the victim afraid . . . for the child like a slave . . . for the land that
longs for rain'. And all of this is set within the context of a funky
latin groove – perhaps a little tricky for some worship bands, but
certainly expressing the joy and celebration which should go
alongside such a faithful, saving God!

Praise in the scattered place

Our final reminder is that praise does not only have to happen
within gathered worship. As Alan and Eleanor Kreider put it:
'Throughout the week as well as at [church] worship, the
Christian is a praising person.'[13] Aspects of our time in church
should remind the congregation members that they can also
praise God out on their frontlines. Does your gathered
worship inspire people to glorify God in the way we speak to
our friends, families and co-workers about what God has done
in our lives? To praise him with the work of our hands, and
the choices we make?

Ideas to try: 'Take My Life' and other songs

The hymn 'Take My Life and Let It Be'[14] by Frances Ridley Havergal
is very effective in this way. It commits the singers to praising God
ceaselessly, and then unpacks various aspects of this: our hands
and feet; our voices; our money; our intellects, our wills and our
hearts. There are a number of versions of this song if you want an

updated musical setting,[15] or alternatives such as 'I Will Offer Up My Life'[16] and 'Before You I Kneel (A Worker's Prayer)'.[17]

We can praise God in our everyday lives and, amazingly, our actions can also inspire unbelievers to do the same. In Matthew 5:16 Jesus instructs us: 'Let your light shine before others, that they may see your good deeds and glorify your Father in heaven.' In order to draw attention to this, you could read out this Bible verse, alongside a modern hymn such as 'Christ Be Our Light',[18] the children's song 'Shine'[19] or the upbeat 'I Love You, Lord (Joy)'.[20] Our deeds within the world, whether that be our work, our care, our giving or even simply the way we treat other people, can be ways of letting the light of Christ shine through our whole lives.

9. BIBLE READING

> This is the true story of Christ that inspires the
> greatest praise and that changed the whole world.
>
> Christopher Voke[1]

Worshipping with the Bible

Many Christians will tell you how important the Bible is
in their faith. Yet take a moment to consider: how much
Scripture is actually read in your gathered services? Are verses
picked out simply to support sermon points? Are particular
books and passages common favourites, while others are
ignored? And if you do read a good proportion of Scripture,
are the members of the congregation helped to engage
with it creatively, reflectively, and in the light of their whole
lives?

This matters because, as we've said in chapter 1, gathered
worship is forming us. If we do not read from and engage
with the breadth of Scripture – God's big story of creation,
fall, Israel, Christ, the early church and our future hope – then
we are in danger of being formed by the stories of this world.
Alan and Eleanor Kreider point out that

> All people are story-shaped; and we Christians especially need
> to be consciously shaped by our alternative story because it is
> an odd story, decisively different from the dominant stories of
> our time . . . We must tell this story so that we know it deeply
> and indwell it, and so that it serves as the lens through which
> we see and evaluate all other stories.[2]

We live in an increasingly biblically illiterate culture, where we
cannot assume that our congregations are familiar with the
whole sweep of God's Word. To live faithful lives on our frontlines we need to be saturated with God's wider story.[3] This
means being intentional about how we read and engage with
the Bible on a weekly basis. That will include dwelling on
longer passages of Scripture, but also the use of shorter verses
and phrases, dropped in along the journey of the service (see
examples below). In this way, congregation members will be
equipped to live for God when they go out into their lives of
scattered worship.

Scripture and creativity

There is a wealth of evocative, inspiring ways to engage with
Scripture. The Bible itself is highly creative. It is made up of
many genres: poetry, song, narrative, letter, gospel, prophecy,
lists, and more. Why treat them all the same way, reading the
Bible as if it were simply a dusty history book?

The people in the Bible heard from God in a huge variety
of multisensory ways. Think, for example, of the dramatic
actions of the prophets or the sounds of the temple musicians.
They communicated to one another in stories and songs,
actions and symbols, poems and prayers.[4] It was only much
later that these were written down. John says in his first letter:
'That which was from the beginning, which we have *heard*,
which we have *seen with our eyes*, which we have *looked at* and

our *hands have touched* – this we proclaim concerning the Word
of life' (1 John 1:1, emphasis ours).

How can we follow in this rich heritage by planning worship
which facilitates an entering into the biblical story, touching
it, tasting it, feeling and living it?

Ideas to try: longer readings – multisensory engagement

One way to bring longer Bible readings to life is to use one of the
five senses, in addition to the sound of the words being read.
The more senses you use in worship, the more experiential it
becomes. As you consider your passage, what sense does it
suggest? Below are some examples, but the opportunities are
endless.

- Touch: is there an item the congregation members could hold
  while listening to the text: a mustard seed (Matthew 17:20) or
  a stone (John 8:7)? Or the object could make a connection with
  their daily lives; for example, get them to hold their mobile
  phones while reading the passage about taming the tongue
  (James 3:3–12). Or invite them to put a sticker inside their shoe
  with Romans 10:15 printed on it, so that on Monday morning,
  when they put their shoes on, they are reminded of this text.
- Sight: you can project images, show a video or use large
  props which bring the text to life. To connect with your
  frontlines you could project photos of your own town or city
  while reading about Jesus weeping over Jerusalem (Luke
  19:41). When hearing about Jesus welcoming little children
  (Luke 18:15–17) you could display the school uniforms from
  all the local schools. Or while reflecting on the prosperity of
  the city (Jeremiah 29:7), you could be looking at images of
  local businesses, community centres and councils.
- Smell: imagine setting up bread-makers around the church to
  coincide with a reading about the bread of life. Or to relate to

whole-life discipleship, use perfume to reflect on
2 Corinthians 2:14–16, where Paul calls us to 'spread the
aroma of the knowledge of [Christ] everywhere'.

- Hearing: sound is highly evocative. Instrumental music, both
recorded and live, can be used to draw out the emotional
impact of a particular Bible passage. Sound effects can also
help congregation members enter into a reading and connect
it to their everyday lives. For example, you could record
the ambient noise of your local high street, and use it to
accompany the reading of Mark 6:34 where Jesus has
compassion on the crowd.

- Taste: the Passover and Lord's Supper both give us great
examples of food being used to communicate God's truth.
What other passages suggest eating something? We have
used bitter tastes like coffee beans to reflect on biblical
lament (e.g. Ezra 10:1), and sweet tastes like honey and
chocolate to experience texts of biblical joy (Psalm 19:10).
Are there tastes associated with people's frontlines,
such as a cuisine of a particular community living in your
area, or a local speciality you could tie in to a Scripture
reading?

Local church story

'We like to take our gathered worship with our young
people outside the church building. We'll take a Bible story
and try and set it in a different environment in our town.
So if Jesus is talking to teachers, we'll go and stand outside
their school, or we'll go out on to the high street, or into
the fields nearby. This brings the Bible stories "home" by
taking them somewhere else.'
Tom, youth worker, Methodist/United Reformed

Ideas to try: longer readings – creative writing and drama
There is something very powerful about a passage of Scripture
being read 'simply' – by someone who has prepared the
reading carefully and prayerfully. Delving deeper into the text
will allow a reader to make decisions about tone of voice, pace
and emphasis, leading to a much more engaging communication
of God's word. The reader can take his or her time over the
words and allow them to sink in. This practice should not be
sidelined.

In addition to this kind of reading, we can also help
congregations engage with Scripture by bringing creative writing
skills and dramatic performance to the service.

Again, the possibilities here are endless, but we would like to
share a few ideas:

- Bob Hartman writes a weekly paraphrase of a Bible text
  (based on the Revised Common Lectionary) which he posts
  on the AREA 52 page of the engageworship.org website.[5]
  He uses a variety of writing techniques: repetition, actions,
  reimagining the story from another character's perspective,
  rhyme, humour, and more.
- As well as using Bob's material, you can learn from him and
  then write your own. Your congregation could view the
  scripture text through the lens of your local context and
  frontlines – what would the feeding of the five thousand
  (Matthew 14:13–21) sound like if set in your local shopping
  centre? What would the parable of the workers (Matthew
  20:1–16) be like in a local business?
- A drama group could imagine the text played by a variety of
  characters. Again, there is the potential that these could be
  brought 'up to date' within your own local community –
  what is the contemporary equivalent of the priest, the Levite
  and the Samaritan from Luke 10:29–37?

Ideas to try: longer readings – reflection

Another aspect that has been lost in many churches is to give
the congregation space and time to reflect on Scripture, whether
it has just been read out loud, displayed on a screen or provided
on a printed sheet. We often rush to hear the preacher explain
it to us, without providing quiet, engaging opportunities for the
Holy Spirit to speak to people through the text.

There are a number of ideas you can use for this:

- Silence. At the Taizé community in France,[6] short passages
  of Scripture are followed by long silences. You could try this
  or ask reflective questions around a Bible reading, leaving
  silence for the congregation members to relate the passage
  to their own lives.
- *Lectio Divina*. This is a traditional monastic approach to
  reading Scripture,[7] which can be led from the front of church
  to help a congregation go deeper into a text. You read or
  hear the passage multiple times, asking God to highlight a
  particular word or phrase. You then invite the members of
  the congregation to chew on (or meditate, ruminate on)
  that word or phrase, asking God to take them deeper into it.
  The third stage is to invite them to shape that word into a
  response – in praise, questions, confession, intercession or
  other appropriate prayers. Finally, you rest in God's presence.
  If a congregation becomes used to this kind of scriptural
  reflection, the members will be able to take it out into their
  own lives and frontlines.
- Scribble sheets. Recently we have been creating sheets with
  the readings printed on them. We have dotted questions
  around the text, and explained that these are not 'test'
  questions but starters for reflection and prayer with God.
  The congregation members can then scribble their prayers,
  responses and doodles all over the sheets, in silence or with

quiet background music. Again, you are equipping the people to engage with the Bible for themselves when they leave church.[8]

If you want to turn these away from being purely individual exercises, we recommend inviting people to come together in small groups after Bible reflection, to share, ask one another questions, and pray for each other. For practical tips on small groups in gathered worship, see appendix 2.

Ideas to try: shorter readings

As well as longer readings, it is helpful to drop shorter verses or sentences from Scripture into your gathered worship. This roots the whole journey in the grammar of God's story. Examples of how you can do this include the following:

- If you are singing a song that quotes from (or alludes to) the Bible, you can read that text during the introduction or musical interlude. This helps the congregation see where that song is rooted.
- You might also let people know about the scripture's context. For example, it is illuminating to realize that the hymn 'Great Is Thy Faithfulness'[9] and the song 'The Steadfast Love of the Lord Never Ceases'[10] both come from the middle of the book of Lamentations. Someone coming in to the service with a heavy heart can find it encouraging that people in the Bible also experienced seasons of brokenness, and expressed these before God while trusting in his faithfulness.
- You can introduce a particular aspect of worship with an appropriate Bible phrase. Confession could be set up with the words from 1 John 1:9, while intercession for the world or your local community could be preceded by James 5:16b.

- Make connections with the congregation's frontlines by reading verses throughout the service that remind us of God's calling on our whole lives. For example, encourage people in their scattered worship with verses like 1 Corinthians 15:58: 'Therefore, my dear brothers and sisters, stand firm. Let nothing move you. Always give yourselves fully to the work of the Lord, because you know that your labour in the Lord is not in vain.'

Integration with preaching

We have already said that we feel that the subject of preaching and whole-life discipleship deserves a book of its own, so we have not included it as a section in this volume. However, at this point we would like to encourage two groups of people, especially in relation to how the Bible is read and reflected on.

- Leaders of music, creativity and services: do all you can to integrate with the preacher. Ask for information about his or her texts and themes as early as you can. Assist in bringing the texts and topics to life through music, art, multisensory ideas and reflection. Enquire as to what might be a helpful approach to the sermon, and also what would be appropriate to follow the talk. This does not mean you have to theme every aspect of the service around the preaching, but it does imply that the whole service follows a logical journey where the music, prayer, activities and sermon are all working together.
- Preachers: do all you can to integrate with the other aspects of the service. Give information to worship leaders a long time in advance of the service. Make suggestions of songs and activities that could usefully

surround the talk, but avoid dictating these aspects. Make connections in your sermons with both the gathered worship of your church and the different ways people can continue this out in their scattered worship. Unpack biblical themes in ways that will expand the congregation's appreciation of whole-life worship.

As you can see, we are encouraging integration between the preacher and the worship leader. If your current context is characterized more by isolation (or even distrust or antagonism), we have some suggestions in chapter 17 for how to develop a sense of teamwork.

By engaging in longer and shorter readings, using creative and varied methods, and integrating well with the sermon, we can saturate our congregations in God's Word and prepare people for fruitful lives of worship on their frontlines.

10. CORPORATE PRAYER

Also, seek the peace and prosperity of the city to
which I have carried you into exile. Pray to the LORD
for it, because if it prospers, you too will prosper.

Jeremiah 29:7

Standing in the need of prayer

Times of corporate prayer within a worship service provide
natural connection points between our scattered and gathered
existence. This should be an easy place to connect with what
is happening in our daily lives. Unfortunately, many churches
have sidelined, or altogether removed, corporate prayer
within worship services. Others may have limited their prayers
to a narrow range of subjects: only praying for the health of
church members, a missionary far away or a particular church
ministry.

The reality is that we are probably less in the habit of
praying for the people and the situations on our frontline than
we are for church-based activities. And that's perhaps because
we don't hear many other prayers in church for frontlines. But
the Lord is no less interested in those situations, those people
or in you when you are there. Bring it all to the Lord in prayer.[1]

As leaders and planners of worship, we may well need to work towards a culture change in the area of corporate prayer. If we can find ways to repeatedly incorporate prayers that include the congregation's frontlines in different ways, eventually it will become the 'new normal'.

John Witvliet suggests that as we engage with this kind of prayer in church, it shapes us for how we live in the world outside. He uses the example of watching tragic news footage and experiencing a sense of powerlessness. Rather than despairing, we can draw from what we have learned in church, turning to God to say, 'Lord, have mercy.'[2] Mark Earey tells the story of Lucy, who discovered that her home-church's inclusion of intercessions each week had shaped her heart for the world: 'She realised that her passionate concern for justice in the world . . . had come, not from sermons, but from years of exposure to public prayer for the poor and oppressed.'[3]

Ideas to try: the sung way of praying

In a 'new church' or 'free church' tradition, corporate prayer may not be a regular part of the service. Many of these churches might have a midweek prayer meeting instead, but if our experience is anything to go by, these are rarely as well attended as the main Sunday service. If you do decide that corporate prayer is important, you may struggle to fit it into the free-flowing style of worship that most charismatic churches favour. This is the first problem.

The second problem in churches with long times of sung worship is that many worshippers seem to have an on–off engagement switch, which appears to be connected to whether music is playing or not. We have certainly experienced that if we stop the music and ask people to sit for a time of prayer, many of them immediately 'switch off'.

A solution to both these problems is to incorporate intercessory prayer within the sung worship. There are plenty of songs to

choose from which either set up the need for prayer or provide
a refrain for prayers (for example, 'Kingdom Coming'[4] or 'O Lord,
Hear My Prayer'[5]). You can suggest subjects for people to pray
about during instrumental sections of the songs or show images
and prayer points on a screen. Members of the congregation
could be invited to pray silently, or all out loud at once, or to
turn to a neighbour and pray, depending on your church's
comfort zone.

Alternatively, you can use songs that are in themselves prayers,
for example, 'Lord, You Hear the Cry',[6] which we mentioned in
chapter 4, or 'King of Compassion'.[7] Sue Rinaldi has said of this
second song:

> I looked out, and I thought: 'How do we put into song these
> troubled times, people who are being bought and sold, the
> whole migrant crisis, the exile, the killing fields?' So I have
> actually tried to put these things into a song, and it is really
> a litany, it is a lament: 'in all these situations, God have mercy!'
> Then follows an anthemic, uplifting chorus to say that God *is*
> the King of Compassion, and that in all these situations, God
> doesn't turn away.[8]

These are the kinds of songs that can stand alone as a powerful
time of intercession, calling out to God for desperate situations
that we might not normally mention in church.

At other times, you might use only one line or phrase to help
you pray. Sam has added tunes to some simple sung phrases for
use in intercession.[9] We often ask everyone in the congregation
to picture a situation, a person or a place in their mind, someone
or somewhere that needs God's help. We then encourage
them to sing the phrase, such as 'O come, o come, Emmanuel'
or 'Send your blessing, Lord', out over the situation they are
picturing.

These ideas will work best if you take a moment to create a seamless flow between songs, for example, by matching the keys or using a subtle modulation.

Local church story

'It is very easy for a lot of worship to become quite inward-looking, but corporate prayer is a chance for us to reframe the way we see our city and our communities. Certainly in the current situation with refugees in Europe, we have found that people in our church have said their eyes have been opened to the reality of that situation because we have prayed for it in church. And this has caused them to rethink how they live their everyday lives, Monday to Saturday.'

Tim, worship leader, Chinese Church

Ideas to try: the low-tech way of praying

A simple, low-tech way of doing this is to make a habit of inviting members of the congregation to share their frontline experiences in front of the whole church. This is known in many churches as 'This Time Tomorrow'.[10] Invite a congregation member up to the front and ask him (or her) practical, frontline-focused questions. What does he do in his everyday life; say, at 10 am on a Monday morning? What is he thankful for in that situation, and what is his greatest challenge? What can the church pray for? Lead the congregation in a prayer, making sure to pray for the actual issues the person has mentioned, rather than dressing it up in super-spiritual language. You could also ask everyone who relates to this person's particular frontline – perhaps they too are teachers or carers and so on – to stand up and be prayed for.

The visual way of praying

As we saw in the previous chapter, the more senses we include in an activity, the more engaging it will be. We are used to being communicated with visually all the time; rarely is any piece of information or entertainment presented to us without pictures, still or moving. To simply ask someone to pray for a war-torn country, for example, or their workplace, may inspire some response, but coupled with photos or some other visual representation, our engagement levels rise. To see your office block, in all its grey dullness, there on the screen in church, where there might normally be sunsets and mountaintops, will hopefully trigger a prayerful response.

Ideas to try: photography

As it is, many people carry a camera around with them, in the form of a smartphone, so here is a chance to get interactive with your prayers. Why not ask your congregation members to take photos in the week of something in the community to pray for, and send them in before Sunday? You could suggest a theme, for example, 'broken' or 'hope', or you could set everyone the challenge to photograph exactly what they are doing at a particular time in the week. This is an opportunity to involve those who do not want to lead worship or prayers up front, but who could influence the prayers of the church in this way. For more on using digital images in church, see appendix 3.

Our favourite experience of using congregation members' photos for prayer happened when we lived in rural Cambridgeshire. Josh, a teenager in the church, had been tasked as part of his A-level course in photography with taking photos of the local area. He could have taken photos of the idyllic countryside where we lived or, perhaps most predictably, the colleges and chapels of Cambridge. Instead, he chatted with and photographed the homeless *Big Issue* sellers gracing the street corners of the picture-perfect city. The photos were stunning and profound, and all we had to do was to find a way to include them in worship. The pictures ended up being installed in the back of our church in a gallery to inform our prayers. There was something so stirring about stopping and looking straight into the eyes of these people, whom we often passed hurriedly on our way to get our shopping. For some people in our village, this may have been the first time they felt any empathy with a homeless person, and it moved us to pray.

Ideas to try: interactive craft

Corporate prayer also lends itself to creative ideas like collage or mosaic. There is something powerful about each individual member of the congregation adding something that represents his or her prayer, and when put together with everybody else's becomes a beautiful picture. This could be done using different green and blue hues of paper to create an image of the earth, or a variety of coloured cellophane, stuck together in front of a window to create a stained-glass effect.[11]

Another idea is to create cityscapes of prayer. Either cut generic cityscapes out of paper, or ask people to cut out a silhouette representing their workplace, home or the area that they see as their frontline. After some time of writing or drawing prayers for these places, stick the cityscapes together and display them in your worship space. Each individual frontline is now joined together and held up in prayer.

Local church story
'As part of our ministry with Resonance Arts we will pray, for example, for the nation of Iran, and have statistics that

detail the situation of the persecuted church there. We will then go on to sing a song in Farsi and in English, which has originated from Iran and that can really connect a congregation with believers in that particular country, under so much persecution.'
David, <www.resonancearts.net>

In the hardest times

Perhaps we avoid praying for some of the more difficult issues because we struggle to find a way to bring them to God in prayer. We simply do not have the vocabulary. But even in a church that hardly ever prays for local or global issues, people will at some point wake up to a horrendous news story one Sunday morning, or have a local tragedy happen in their area or church community, and will know that it has to be mentioned somehow.

The first thing to do is to draw comfort, as well as language, from Scripture. The Bible does not shy away from real suffering; it shows people in pain and it shows a God who cares. The Psalms, especially, are rich in lament. We can mourn along with the psalmist: 'How long will the enemy mock you, God? Will the foe revile your name for ever?' (Psalm 74:10) or 'LORD, you are the God who saves me; day and night I cry out to you. May my prayer come before you; turn your ear to my cry' (Psalm 88:1) and so on. Consider how you could pray the language of the Psalms to face up to terrible situations.

Second, we can find language and inspiration from sisters and brothers who have gone before us. The 'spirituals' from the black church tradition in the USA are one example; many of these songs were able to express deep despair over the situation the community found itself in, while also trusting in God faithfully. As Graham Cray says: 'there is a tension in the spirituals, perfectly expressed in the musical form, between present pain and certain hope. Between hope for eternity, but also hope for the present.'[12]

Ideas to try: songs of pain and hope

We recommend Geraldine and Carey Luce's two albums of spirituals for choirs, which can be easily picked up by a church.[13] In this context, the simple song 'The Needy Will Not Be Forgotten'[14] with its repeated refrain 'There is a God who sees' contains especially helpful words for the most difficult moments.

Further back in church history, one of the earliest Christian prayers is *Kyrie Eleison* (Greek for 'Lord, have mercy'). There are many musical settings of these words,[15] or you can make up your own tune. Or in a really desperate situation it might be best to leave silence, and then simply say the words 'Lord, have mercy' as you hold the pain of the world before God.

As we step into praying for our world and our frontlines regularly, creatively and honestly, we will find that what we do in church provides a vocabulary and inspiration for the congregation to remain prayerful in their daily lives, whatever they are facing.

---

11. CONFESSION OF SIN

God's forgiveness is deeper than our sinfulness.
Through confession . . .
Christians are formed by grace.

Stanley Hauerwas and Samuel Wells[1]

The hardest word?

Nobody likes saying 'sorry'. As parents, we struggle to get our children to apologize. But if we are honest, it is something that most adults struggle with too! No wonder that confession of sin is something that many worship planners avoid. They may consider it off-putting to 'seekers'; it could remind people of manipulative leadership or simply be seen as something of a 'downer'. However, if this is the case then we have confused what Paul calls 'worldly sorrow' with what confession can and should be: life-giving 'godly sorrow'.

> Godly sorrow brings repentance that leads to salvation and leaves no regret, but worldly sorrow brings death. See what this godly sorrow has produced in you: what earnestness, what eagerness to clear yourselves, what indignation, what alarm, what longing, what concern, what readiness to see justice done.
> (2 Corinthians 7:10–11)

Being honest about our failures, speaking them out before God and receiving his endless forgiveness is a powerful and transformative process. Saying sorry and receiving God's grace are at the heart of the gospel. Confession allows us to deal with the mistakes we have made on our frontlines, and forms us to be a people who daily turn to God for restoration.

This is true for individuals, for our secret sins and personal problems. But if we do include confession in gathered worship, we ought to be careful that it is not limited to being 'an inward-looking and individualistic act'.[2] Corporate confession, for wider issues in our church, community and society, should also be included. We can reinforce the dualism of the sacred–secular divide if we never admit to the ways in which our lives fall short of what we sing and pray about in church. We should learn from the people of God in the Old Testament, who regularly had to come back to God and say as a body: '*We* have sinned, even as our ancestors did; *we* have done wrong and acted wickedly' (Psalm 106:6, emphasis ours).

An example of this can be found in Isaiah 58. The Israelites are going through all the religious motions of fasting and humility (vv. 3, 5). Yet their sin is in how they relate to their workers (v. 3b); how they treat one another (v. 4); how they oppress their slaves (v. 6); and how they ignore the hungry, homeless and naked (v. 7). Isaiah calls them to repent of how they live in the world, to turn around and live differently in the scattered place, so that their prayers in the gathered place will be heard and their 'light will break forth like the dawn, and [their] healing will quickly appear' (v. 8).[3]

Ideas to try: written confession prayers

In order to help congregations with this, we have written prayers of confession, and surrounded them with relevant songs and imagery.[4] One prayer is based on the theme of our gathered worship not matching up to our actions of justice and mercy in the world. It could be included in a journey of worship, using songs like 'God of Justice'[5] or 'King of Compassion'.[6]

[Leader] Father, when our worship has been more about us than about you,

[All] **Lord, have mercy.**

When our songs have ignored the pain of your broken body on earth,

Christ, have mercy.

When our services have been more of an escape for us, than good news to the poor,

Lord, have mercy.

When we praise you with our lips, but deny you with our finances,

Christ, have mercy.

When our instruments are louder than our cries for justice,

Lord, have mercy.

When we fail to learn from the sacrificial worship of brothers and sisters across the world,

Christ, have mercy.[7]

Another area for corporate repentance is in how we have treated God's creation. As Christopher Voke says: 'An urgent need in the contemporary church is for regular inclusion in public worship of confession . . . about the environment.'[8] You can set this up in a journey with songs about the beauty of God's creation ('Indescribable',[9] 'How Great Thou Art',[10] 'Praise Him You Heavens'[11]), and then potentially use the hymn 'God in Such Love for Us'[12] (mentioned in chapter 6) as a pivot into thinking about how we have misused the planet. We have then shown images of environmental damage (both globally and locally), encouraging

people to reflect on their own attitude towards stewarding God's
world. Finally, we have said this prayer together:

[*Leader*] Lord, when we have taken your creation for granted;
[*All*]   **forgive us, gracious Father.**
          When we have abused its resources and polluted its
          purity;
          forgive us, gracious Father.
          When we have not fulfilled our calling to steward your
          earth;
          forgive us, gracious Father.

          [Invite the congregation to silently receive God's
          forgiveness.]

          May we work with you in the renewal of creation;
          empower us, Holy Spirit.
          May we speak and act for the good of your planet;
          inspire us, Jesus Christ.
          May we value and share the good gifts you provide;
          encourage us, Father of creation. Amen.[13]

Assurance of forgiveness

It is important when we lead a confession prayer that this is
followed with a reminder that the congregation is forgiven by
God (sometimes called 'absolution' or 'assurance of pardon').[14]
This can be done by speaking out the truth from Scripture of
God's grace and mercy (e.g. Psalm 103:12; Acts 13:38). Clayton
Schmit writes: 'Words of absolution are among the most
powerful and meaningful spoken in worship. They indicate
the good news of the gospel in concrete and immediate
terms.'[15]

Ideas to try: song and actions for forgiveness

As well as spoken words, there are other ways to communicate forgiveness. A song after a confession prayer can be very powerful, for example 'I'm Forgiven (You Are My King)',[16] Chris Tomlin's chorus to 'Amazing Grace',[17] or even the simple 1980s song 'I'm Accepted'.[18]

Beyond words and songs, physical movement can help us enact repentance and receive forgiveness. You could write a confession prayer down and then destroy it in some way: put it in a paper shredder, throw it in a bonfire or wipe it off a whiteboard. Prayers can be written with a finger in sand (echoing Jesus in John 8:6–8) and then erased. Or an object can represent a sin; for example, encourage the congregation members to hold their bunch of keys, and reflect on their attitude towards home, hospitality and welcome. They could confess any sins of selfishness in this way, and then be given a key ring which reminds them of God's call to welcome strangers (Hebrews 13:2).

Local church story

'The chants of the Taizé community are often sung repeatedly into a time of silent prayer. Into that silence you bring all the knowledge of the community's commitment to peace, justice and reconciliation, and that can be applied to praying for your own particular situation.'
Anne, freelance church musician and educator, Church of England

Reconciliation with others

A final thought for this section is that confession ought to go hand in hand with reconciliation, forgiving other people and attempting to restore relationships. J. G. Davies notes that in the Lord's Prayer, 'forgive us our sins' is immediately followed by 'as we forgive those who sin against us'. He suggests that 'the ministry of reconciliation, which is at the heart of mission, is inseparably bound up with the essential meaning of confession and absolution in worship'.[19] As we grow in relationship and forgiveness within our church family, we are being equipped to be agents of reconciliation in our daily lives. We can take this attitude into our struggles with our boss, a difficult customer or an obstinate neighbour.

Jesus taught (Matthew 5:23–24) that if we are coming to worship, and remember an unresolved issue with a brother or sister, we should reconcile before we continue to offer our sacrifice. Anabaptists Alan and Eleanor Kreider have traced how this became a part of early church worship (what we now know as the sharing of 'the Peace'), where the believers would greet one another and restore any broken relationships as part of their gathered services. This practice faded in later years, but they think we can see it restored within contemporary church as a space for reconciliation.[20]

As we do this with one another, we are anticipating and hastening the time when God will 'reconcile to himself all things, whether things on earth or things in heaven, by making peace through his blood, shed on the cross' (Colossians 1:20).

Ideas to try: reconciliation

- Have a time of 'passing the peace' or greeting, and during the introduction encourage people to consider if there are brothers and sisters in the room they need to go to and forgive, asking for forgiveness from them and being reconciled.
- Sing a song such as Graham Kendrick's 'All the Room Was Hushed and Still',[21] which encourages us to love and serve one another.

- Engage in foot washing or hand washing, where you provide bowls and towels, and make space for people to enact service and reconciliation through this act.

We are aware that there are pastoral issues around this subject which need to be handled sensitively. In particular, things like foot washing are considered by some people to be uncomfortable and difficult. While we have sympathy with this, and encourage you to be careful in giving an opt-out for activities such as foot washing, we also believe that a countercultural act such as this can itself be transformative. Mark Thiessen Nation writes: 'Churches that practice foot washing are likely to be those that are committed to the components of foot washing in their daily lives.'[22] Perhaps physically serving a brother or sister in this way, within church worship, is exactly the kind of thing we need to prepare us for service in our whole lives.

12. TESTIMONY

Here's the story I'll tell my friends
when they come to worship,
and punctuate it with Hallelujahs.

Psalm 22:22, MSG

Frontline stories

In chapter 3 we discussed the importance of a 'revelation' from God inspiring a 'response' from us. Scripture should be our main source for this – it is the place where God's character and actions are revealed to us in detail. But there are other places where we can see God revealed, for example, in his creation and through works of art.

There is, however, little else which is as inspiring as someone's testimony: a real person, who has had a genuine experience of God, declaring it in your hearing. Testimony is also a worshipful response in itself; it is giving God credit for what he has done – it is bringing him glory.

One of the reasons why testimony is so powerful to us is because it can be multidimensional. Here is a brother or a sister (the horizontal dimension), sharing a story that glorifies God (vertical), and often the story is set outside church (third dimension) – God's salvation story just popped into enhanced 3D mode! How sad, then, when testimonies in a church are limited to 2D because people are not encouraged to speak of 'mundane' frontline experiences. In many churches, the only people telling testimonies are those who have been out on a mission trip or perhaps those involved in a church-based outreach ministry. Not only does this practice limit the scope of testimony, but it also forms a particular culture. As Neil Hudson says: 'If the only invited stories are the stories of the church ministry teams, people can quickly draw conclusions as to the roles that are most valued.'[1]

The vast majority of people in church may not be travelling the world, seeing scores come to Christ or arranging healing meetings in the local arena. They do, however, have to decide whether to stand up for truth in a board meeting; they have to receive God's power to extend love and grace to a difficult pupil; or work out how to glorify God in a dead-end job at a fast-food outlet. Let's tell each other these stories, to the glory of God and to build each other up.

Now, the fact that in the past most testimonies have been given by the 'global-evangelist types' may also have something to do with personality. Not everyone loves being the centre of attention on a platform. Some might feel fearful about their voice faltering or using the wrong terminology. As leaders and planners of worship, we should find ways to help people bring glory to God through testimony without having to have a personality transplant.

Ideas to try: testimony interspersed with singing

We regularly hand out small slips of paper and pens before or in the early stages of a service. There might be a question on there or we might put a question on the screen; for example, 'What is one way where you've seen God's goodness this week?' If your church is familiar with the frontline language, you may want to ask for things that God has specifically done or how he has shown himself to be on their frontlines. For this particular worship activity, brevity is helpful, so make the slips small to discourage essays (for some people, a large, blank sheet of paper may also seem daunting).

We then collect the slips and spend a moment sorting them into sections, ensuring that the ones about runaway cats returning and those about miraculous healings are evenly spread out, not elevating one over the other. Within a suitable song, we intersperse responsive singing with reading the testimonies aloud, while the music continues at a lower volume. Any song that praises God is appropriate here: the choruses of 'How Great Is Our God'[2] and 'Our God Is an Awesome God'[3] are both helpful, but choose one from your church's repertoire. If you are a worship leader leading from an instrument, you will need to delegate the testimony reading to a singer or service leader. These are holy moments, when those who do not normally share receive an opportunity to help lead the worship with their honest stories. Within the safety of relative anonymity (depending perhaps on the size of your community), you will be surprised at the depth in which people share.

A simpler, but similar, way to 'crowdsource' testimonies is to ask everyone in the beginning of a sung worship time to close their eyes and think of one thing that they are thankful to God for. We then typically sing 'Give Thanks to the Lord Our God and King',[4] all the way through and then stay on a G-chord and ask if people are willing to speak out the particular things that they are thankful for. Perhaps using a roving mic, people get a chance to say their one thing, while the congregation responds after each one with the refrain which we have just used in the song: 'His love endures forever.' We may then sing the chorus again to finish. It is a wonderful thing to hear many different people's voices thanking and glorifying God in this way for things that have happened during daily life.

Ideas to try: I was . . . but now I am . . .

In John 9 we find the remarkable story of a healed ex-blind man being pressurized by the Pharisees to renounce Jesus. The undeniable fact of this man's healing was a testimony in itself, but the Pharisees were upset that the glory seemed to be going to Jesus, in their eyes a mere man. 'Give glory to God!' they demand of the man, reiterating that they believed Jesus to be a sinner. The man responds, 'Whether he is a sinner or not, I don't know. One thing I do know. I was blind but now I see!' (9:25).

Sometimes we may not feel able to share eloquently about exactly how God has worked in our lives, but we, like the man healed from blindness, know the results. This is when telling testimonies based on John 9:25 is both helpful and powerful. There are many filmed examples online of churches that have done this using cardboard (search for 'cardboard testimonies'). One side of the cardboard has the 'I was . . .' part written on it, and the other side has 'but now I am . . .' As it is turned over, you see, for example, 'I was lonely, but now I am part of the family of God.'

When we wanted to try this in our church, we knew that many people would not want to take part when they found out that it would involve standing up front and flipping cardboard over dramatically. Instead, we printed out small slips which said, 'I was . . .' and a few spaces down 'but now I am . . .' We explained the concept to the whole congregation before giving people some time to write. When we collected up the slips, we were floored by the openness and depth of these simple testimonies. Who would have thought our average, middle-England Baptist church contained such powerful testimonies? These transformations, read out in a worshipful context, reduced many of us to tears.

One of the helpful things about this way of telling testimony is the way it equips and prepares us for our frontlines. 'Always be prepared to give an answer to everyone who asks you to give the reason for the hope that you have. But do this with gentleness and respect,' writes Peter (1 Peter 3:15). Many people outside church may not be interested in long theological discourses, and Peter warns us about bullying people into faith, but who can resist a 'I was . . . but now I am . . .' story?

Direct frontline links

With a bit of preparation and forward planning, it is possible to make a direct link to people's frontlines, right there in the worship space on a Sunday morning. On a weekday, you could meet a congregation member at her (or his) workplace, social club, by the school gates or wherever she identifies as her main frontline. Photograph or film her there, and ask her to share how she has experienced God's faithfulness in that particular place. This can then be shown during gathered worship.

One of the benefits of this is that it moves us away from testimony only being about success stories. Congregation members can get discouraged if they only hear positive conclusions from the front of church. It can actually be heartening to hear that other people are struggling, or that not all prayers are answered in the way we anticipate. So encourage an atmosphere of openness and truth-telling within your frontline stories, even if you have to set the tone yourself by admitting to some of the harder aspects of your life.

To create a habit of sharing frontline testimonies, encourage the use of social media. You could announce a Twitter hashtag, for example, #frontlinemiracles, and ask worshippers to tweet throughout the week when they spot something that God is doing. Alternatively, you could start a Facebook group for sharing stories, and these can make their way into the gathered worship.

13. OFFERING

We give our whole life;
God should have ownership of everything.

John Wimber[1]

The gift of giving

'The offering bag will be passed around during this song. This is just for church members to contribute to the running of our church, so if you are a visitor please let the bag pass by . . .' This is the often-heard 'liturgy' in many churches around taking a collection. In other congregations, the offering has been entirely replaced by a plate at the back of church or an encouragement to set up a standing order.

The emphasis here is on a) avoiding the impression that the church is just after your money, and b) keeping the financial wheels of the church spinning. Of course, neither of these aims is bad or unimportant in itself. But they both miss a great opportunity to connect the gathered worship of the church with the congregation's frontline existence.

In a context where gathered worship is often overly spiritu-alized, dualistic and detached from physical reality, the giving of money, resources and time as an act of worship is an ideal corrective. This has been a part of worship since biblical times – clearly in the tithes and offerings of the Old Testament, but also in the teaching of Jesus (Matthew 25:37–40) and in Paul's collection for the Jerusalem church (2 Corinthians 8 – 9).

There are still contexts today where a collection continues to be a life-giving gathered-worship practice – we hear stories of the exuberant giving in some non-Western churches where people dance their way to the offering plate. And some versions of Vineyard founder John Wimber's five-phase flow of worship (mentioned in chapter 5) culminate in 'the giving of substance'.[2] How can we learn from these examples, while avoiding a 'prosperity gospel' message or an over-emphasis on money?

We want to suggest four theological angles that can be creatively emphasized within times of offering:[3]

1. All good gifts come from God.
2. All worship and service is a grateful 'giving back'.
3. What we give in gathered worship can be a symbol of our wider giving.
4. Our giving is partnering with God in the renewal of all things.

These can lift what could otherwise simply be an administrative task to become a worshipful and whole-life response.

1. All good gifts come from God

'The earth is the LORD's, and everything in it' proclaims Psalm 24:1, while James reminds us that 'Every good and perfect gift is from above' (James 1:17). We may need to help the congregation to see that this includes 'everyday' things: money, jobs, possessions and leisure time. A time of offering in church can be a way of reminding ourselves that all we have, in every sphere, has been provided by God and ultimately belongs to him.

Ideas to try: wallet prayer

Carol Penner suggests a tactile way to encourage people to meditate on this. Around a time of offering she encourages those in the congregation to use their wallet or purse as a symbol of what God has given to them, reflecting on it with the following prayer:

> We are entirely yours God;
> life, and breath, and heart, and soul.
> We hold our wallets in our hands;
> we find here the power to buy,
> and the power to give.
> All power we have is a gift from you.
> We give this offering generously
> in the spirit of Christ
> who gave heart and soul and mind and strength to you,
> freely and with deep love. Amen.[4]

Ideas to try: harvest festival

Harvest festivals may seem outdated in the twenty-first century, especially in an urban church, but they can be reimagined and provide a vital link to the places where we work – paid or unpaid. You could invite everyone to bring an object that represents what God produces through them (not necessarily to be given away). This could include cakes, reports, digital devices, photos of people who are cared for or managed, pieces of art, school books, manufactured items and so on. These could be brought up to the communion table and placed before God as a symbol of offering, to thank him for working through us and providing for us.[5]

Ideas to try: Celtic prayers

Celtic Christian spirituality also contains resources for helping us remember that God provides in our daily lives. A contemporary expression of this kind can be found in the songs and prayers of the Iona Community, where 'the Celtic sense of the presence of Christ in all of life's activities and encounters is a theme that runs throughout'.[6]

> Generous God,
> we thank you that, time after time, in the most surprising places,
> you spread a table for us
> and welcome us to the feast
> of your presence.
>
> Sometimes we feel like amazed guests
> at a banquet, a great celebration;
> sometimes we meet you at a kitchen table among friends,
> sharing daily bread;
> sometimes as children enjoying a picnic, laughing, singing,
> in the sunshine;
> sometimes in a dark valley, on a hard journey, by the barbed
> wire, bread is broken.
>
> Always we find nourishment;
> always enough for all who come;
> we see that no-one is ever turned away;
> and always we are blessed by sharing –
> this is the gospel feast.
>
> Thank you for such good food,
> giving strength to do your work in the world,
> and for your welcome at our journey's end. Amen.[7]

Could your church include Iona Community or other such Celtic material around your time of offering? Or perhaps you can be inspired by this approach to create similar resources that will connect your people's Sunday worship with their everyday experience of God's provision.

---

2. All worship and service is a grateful 'giving back'

The Christian response of giving, whether in gathered or scattered worship, can never be about earning or trying to buy God's favour. It is always a grateful response to the gospel, an overflow of 'giving back' (however inadequately) for all he has done for us. As we saw in chapter 2, it is in the light of God's mercy (see Paul's whole argument of salvation by grace in Romans 1 – 11) that we are to offer our bodies, our whole selves, as a living sacrifice (Romans 12:1).

How can your songs, prayers and activities around offering emphasize this aspect of giving? There are ways in which you can first remind people of the grace and mercy of God, for example, by reading Ephesians 2:8–10:

> For it is by grace you have been saved, through faith – and this is not from yourselves, it is the gift of God – not by works, so that no one can boast. For we are God's handiwork, created in Christ Jesus to do good works, which God prepared in advance for us to do.

Ideas to try: songs for 'giving back'
Some songs that could bring this out include 'I Will Offer Up My Life',[8] 'When I Survey the Wondrous Cross'[9] and 'In the Light of Your Mercy'. This third song picks up on the message of

Romans 12:1 and then unpacks a breadth of things we offer
back to God:

> In the light of your mercy,
> we offer up our lives,
> all we are, for you.
> In the power of your Spirit
> a living sacrifice,
> all we are, for you.
>
> We bring the work of our hands,
> our dreams and our plans,
> the fruit of our lips,
> our talents and gifts;
> our kindness and care,
> the knowledge we share,
> the money we make,
> all our small steps of faith.
>
> We bring our doubts and our fears,
> our joys and our tears,
> our failings and flaws,
> for you see it all;
> the whole of our lives
> we offer through Christ,
> may our worship be true,
> bringing glory to you.[10]

As you use words like these around times of offering, you can
pray that your hearts will be inspired by God's generosity to be
grateful in our giving back.

3. What we give in gathered worship can be a symbol of our wider giving

We realize that there is a reluctance to 'show off' by giving in overly ostentatious ways. In fact, Jesus warns us against such boasting in Matthew 6:2–4. Yet it remains a powerful symbol to allow members of the congregation to make a physical offering of some kind, which represents the wider giving of their time, talents, money and possessions out on their frontlines.

Ideas to try: gift box response

One way to do this is to hand out slips of paper, and encourage the congregation members to write down how they are going to serve God in the week. You can focus on a particular area of giving: how they will use their time for God's glory or how their work will be an offering to him. This is private, between each person and God. You can then have a 'gift box' prepared, covered in bright wrapping paper and bows. Encourage people to put their pieces of paper into the box as a symbol of what they are planning to give.

Ideas to try: object offering

Another idea is to widen what is given beyond money, by taking collections of physical objects. Churches can invite their congregations to bring non-perishable foods for a local food bank, nappies for struggling young families or presents for a Christmas shoebox appeal.[11] These can be brought forward in an atmosphere of joy and celebration, and a prayer can be said to show that these are symbols of our intention to give all things over to God. It also links in with our final point.

---

4. Our giving is partnering with God in the renewal of all things

In Justin Martyr's account of a very early church service, he describes the offering like this:

> Those who are prosperous and who desire to do so, give what they wish, according to each one's own choice, and the collection is deposited with the presider. He aids orphans and widows, those who are in want through disease or through another cause, those who are in prison, and foreigners who are sojourning here. In short, the presider is a guardian to all those who are in need . . .[12]

From its earliest times, Christian giving has been seen as a way to partner with God in bringing about justice, wholeness and *shalom*. This is not a tacked-on social agenda, but a participation in God's plan to heal and restore the whole of his creation.

Ideas to try: building the kingdom

In your gathered worship you can highlight how the church's offering is making a difference in local and global situations, through testimonies, images and videos. You can also invite congregation members to share how their giving of time, money and possessions on their frontline is ushering in God's kingdom. You could then surround the time of offering with a song that emphasizes our desire to see God transform our community, such as Rend Collective's 'Build Your Kingdom Here'.[13]

Consider how you can creatively and sensitively reimagine a time of offering within your gathered worship, so that it inspires, symbolizes and sends people out to a life of giving and serving in their scattered worship.

14. THE LORD'S TABLE

> The sacraments are a means of grace that God uses
> to call, inspire, and feed disciples for the service and
> proclamation they take into the world.
>
> Clayton Schmit[1]

Transforming table

You may call it the Lord's Supper or Communion, Mass or the
Eucharist; it may be formal and structured or relaxed and
spontaneous; and you might celebrate it once a week, once a
month or once a year. Whatever your pattern, it is easy to miss
the world-changing implications of sharing bread and wine,
giving it 'an introverted orientation that only dwells on the
benefits for believers'.[2]

This meal has every potential to be a radical, transformative
encounter with the living God (vertical), which we share with
our church family (horizontal), in the light of God's re-
creating plan for the whole world (third dimension). We want
to suggest three ways in which the Lord's Table can shape us
for fruitfulness on our frontlines, and give some practical
suggestions for resources and actions that may help you
reframe your celebrations for whole-life worship.

A community of radical hospitality

Public meals in ancient Corinth were an opportunity to show off your social status, to exclude people 'less' than you and elevate your own position. Paul expected the Lord's Supper to be radically countercultural to this trend – one body, by one baptism and one Spirit, with no division on the basis of race or social status (1 Corinthians 12:13). So he was horrified to find disunity and injustice in the eating habits of the church members at Corinth, with the rich getting fat and drunk before the poor had even finished their day's work (1 Corinthians 11:17–23). Alan and Eleanor Kreider comment:

> The Corinthians' way of eating divided members along class and economic lines which, Paul contended, expressed 'contempt for the Church of God.' Instead of honouring all those whom God had called from many social origins to be one in Christ, the Corinthian meals 'humiliate[d] those who have nothing.'[3]

Some churches use 1 Corinthians 11 as an introduction to a time of communion. If you include Paul's exhortation that we should all 'examine ourselves' before taking bread and wine (11:28), you can emphasize that in context he is writing about how we treat those around us. How welcoming and inclusive are we? Do our daily lives reflect Jesus' practice of radical hospitality? He ate with tax collectors and sinners (Luke 15:2) and even shared his Last Supper with the one who would betray him (Luke 22:21). Do our attitudes anticipate our hope for the meal when God will welcome all peoples to his table?

> . . . the LORD Almighty will prepare
> a feast of rich food for all peoples,

a banquet of aged wine –
    the best of meats and the finest of wines.
(Isaiah 25:6)

Could you use Bible passages like this, and perhaps a song like 'Feast on His Love',[4] to encourage the members of the congregation to consider their own life of welcome and hospitality, before they themselves are welcomed to the table?

The words that surround communion are very important in drawing out the breadth of its meaning, but be aware that it is not words alone that convey meaning in this meal. Very practical things like how the chairs are set up, the placement of the communion table, how the elements are distributed and who distributes them can all give an impression of welcome or exclusion. On a very pragmatic note, the availability of alcohol-free wine and gluten-free bread can make a huge difference to those who require them, and the way that these are made available can also either reinforce a sense that you aren't the 'norm' in this church or help to communicate that all are equally welcome.

Archbishop Desmond Tutu was Dean of St Mary's Cathedral, Johannesburg, during the terrible time of segregation in apartheid South Africa. He describes the welcome at that church as a 'total liturgy':

as I have knelt in the Dean's stall at the superb 9.30 High Mass . . . watching a multiracial crowd file up to the altar rails to be communicated, the one bread and the one cup given by a mixed team of clergy and lay ministers with a multiracial choir, servers and sidemen – all this in apartheid-mad South Africa – then tears sometimes streamed down my cheeks, tears of joy that it could be that indeed Jesus Christ had broken down the wall of partition, and here were the first fruits of the eschatological community right in front of my eyes, enacting the message in several languages on the notice-board outside, that this is a house of prayer for people of all races who are welcome at all times.[5]

Think for a moment: could your gathered worship be described as 'total liturgy' or 'total worship', not merely singing and praying for unity, love and justice but demonstrating it in the way you embrace all who come? Are all gifts valued? Are all styles and expressions encouraged? Is every people-group present asked to bring its own contribution?

Ideas to try: song of radical hospitality

To engage the congregation with this concept, perhaps you could sing or listen to Stuart Townend's song 'Vagabonds' as you come to the table:

> Come, all you vagabonds,
> come all you 'don't belongs'
> winners and losers,
> come, people like me.
> Come all you travellers
> tired from the journey,
> come wait a while, stay a while,
> welcomed you'll be.
>
> Come all you questioners
> looking for answers,
> and searching for reasons
> and sense in it all;
> come all you fallen,
> and come all you broken,
> find strength for your body
> and food for your soul.

Come to the feast,
there is room at the table.
Come let us meet in this place
with the King of all kindness
who welcomes us in,
with the wonder of love,
and the power of grace.[6]

The challenge is, after hearing it, does your practice of gathered worship live up to the lyrics?

Physical creation graced by God

Another aspect of the Lord's Supper that relates to our daily lives is that in it we see God working through ordinary, physical objects. This is not a spiritualized, ethereal act of worship, but one rooted in the very everyday stuff of food and drink. It is not an alien ritual but, at its foundation, a shared meal between friends.

This is where it is worth remembering that the Lord's Supper is what some churches call a 'sacrament', an ordinance, a 'means of grace' by which God takes a physical thing and, by his Spirit, communicates something of himself. It is a foretaste and a sign of what God has begun in Jesus Christ, continues to do through his church, and will finally complete when he comes again: the restoration and making new of all things in heaven and on earth. Because of this, Tom Wright is able to say that when we eat the Lord's Supper:

We taste new creation on our tongue, on our lips, in our mouth, in our bodies, so that we can then go out and do new creation in the world: that's how it is meant to work.

Maybe if we get that right we'll be doing more new creation in the world.[7]

If we can reclaim this sense of God working 'sacramentally' through the bread and wine, perhaps we can also see the more everyday 'sacraments' of God working through our chores, our hours at the office, our art and creativity, our conversations and care.

This is what Laura Kelly Fanucci has done in her book *Everyday Sacraments*, as she reflects on her life as a parent through a 'sacramental imagination', concluding: 'the sacraments invite all of us to open our eyes to a wider view in which every moment offers opportunities to encounter God's grace.'[8] Could you unpack this idea in your communion service, with testimonies of how God has worked 'sacramentally' through experiences on people's frontlines?

It could also be that the actual bread and wine you use makes a difference. Eating a liturgical wafer may not suggest the 'everyday' nature of the bread that God chooses to grace. Can you use the kind of bread and wine (or juice) that people recognize from their daily lives so that they make the connections to God's transformative power the next time they make a sandwich or sit down for a drink with friends?

Engaging with a bigger story

We can also consider whether the prayers and songs we use around the Lord's Table are simply about personal salvation, or if they link Christ's death and resurrection with God's bigger story: the making new of all creation. Alan and Eleanor Kreider believe that 'The greatest missed opportunity to tell the big story of God's mission in many churches is surely the thanksgiving prayers at the Lord's Supper'.[9] This should inspire us to play our part in God's plan. In the words of Tom Wright:

> There's a close fit between welcoming and recognizing the Christ who comes to us as the one who fills heaven and earth and who now mysteriously fills this bread and wine, and the Christ who comes to us in the face of those in need whom we meet on the street or elsewhere. My sense is that the sacraments energize us for our work in the world.[10]

Ideas to try: songs and prayers

Consider how these lines from a New Zealand communion prayer express both the universal and personal implications of God's saving plan:

> For with your whole created universe,
> we praise you for your unfailing gift of life.
> Your love is shown to us, for while we were yet sinners,
> Christ died for us.
>
> In that love, dear God,
> righteous and strong to save,
> you came among us in Jesus Christ,
> our crucified and living Lord.
>
> You make all things new.
> In Christ's suffering and cross
> you reveal your glory
> and reconcile all peoples to yourself,
> their true and living God.[11]

There are songs that reflect this angle; 'All Things New' by Red Mountain Music[12] is based on a hymn by Horatius Bonar:

Come, for creation groans,
impatient of Thy stay,
worn out with these long years of ill,
these ages of delay.

Come, and make all things new;
build up this ruined earth;
come and make all things new.[13]

As you come to the end of your gathered time, what better prayer
to send the congregation out to participate in this making new of
all things than these wonderful words from the Anglican Holy
Communion:

Almighty God,
we thank you for feeding us
with the body and blood of your Son Jesus Christ.
Through him we offer you our souls and bodies
to be a living sacrifice.
Send us out
in the power of your Spirit
to live and work
to your praise and glory.
Amen.[14]

May your celebration of communion inspire you to go out and
live and work to God's praise and glory.

15. RESPONSE

Failing to specifically and explicitly invite people to
put the message into action in their lives will simply
produce spiritually fat people, not Jesus followers
ready to face the challenges of this world.

Bob Rognlien[1]

Two-way conversation

Through being married to Sara, I (Sam) have discovered that
if she is speaking to me, I cannot only inwardly acknowledge
her comments and walk away. This does not make for a
fruitful relationship! She wants me to respond – perhaps just
with a nod and a smile or a 'Sorry to hear that'. In particular,
if she is asking me to do something, she wants me to agree
to do it, or discuss the idea, and then get on with it. I might
be a slow learner, but I am gradually realizing the value of
two-way communication.

A time of response towards the end of a service helps
ensure that worship remains a conversation. We hear God's
word – preached, sung, prayed, painted and more – and
then we get the opportunity to consider and commit to
how we are going to react. Constance Cherry points out that
after Peter preached in Acts 2, it was not enough for the

congregation simply to sing a song and go home.[2] The crowd
has an emotional response (2:37); a spiritual response (in this
case, repentance and receiving the Holy Spirit, 2:38); a
symbolic response (being baptized, 2:41); and an action
response ('They devoted themselves to the apostles' teaching
and to fellowship, to the breaking of bread and to prayer . . .
They sold property and possessions to give to anyone who
had need', 2:42–45). How can we facilitate these different
responses within our gathered worship?

Considering our whole-life theme, we have a further strong
mandate to help the members of our congregations reflect
on the impact of the message for their everyday lives. Each
week will require a different kind of response. Planners of
worship need to think and pray about what will be appropriate and necessary in the light of the songs, challenges,
scriptures and teaching that have come before. We should also
consider the situations and settings we know our congregations are heading into. As well as planning, there are times
when we need to be flexible and go with what the Spirit is
doing during the service, rather than doggedly sticking to our
script. Below are some ideas to get you thinking about how
to approach response times.

Ideas to try: reflecting

One of the opportunities we have in a response time is to create
space for reflection. The simplest form would be to ask a few
questions (either verbally or on a screen, or both) which help the
worshippers apply the teaching to their lives, and then leave some
silence or play quiet, instrumental music. Questions might include:

- How does this teaching challenge you in your everyday life?
- What would be one practical step for you to take in applying
  this principle from God's word?

- Who on your frontline do you need to engage with differently, in the light of this message?
- What does this scripture suggest God's perspective is on a difficulty you are facing right now?

Another form of reflection is called the *examen*, from the sixteenth-century Jesuit Ignatius of Loyola.[3] The simplest way to approach it is in three stages:

1. Looking back – what am I most grateful for? (It helps to make this specific: look back at your past week in work or consider your experience of, say, family over the past year.) Talk to God about this.
2. Looking back – what have been the challenges? (Again, you can tie this in to the theme of the teaching.) Talk to God about this.
3. Looking forward – ask God to help you live differently, and walk with him through what is ahead.

This can be done in silence, or you could pass out sheets of paper with questions you want people to ponder, and explain that if it helps they could write their answers down as a kind of 'letter to God'. Not only does this help people process God's word in the light of their everyday lives, but it is also a practice they can take with them on to their frontlines. Ignatius required the Jesuits to pray this at midday and in the evening – it is intended as a way of 'checking in' with God in a busy life.

Because some people process their thoughts in an extrovert way, they may find this quiet, introverted reflection difficult. We have often followed a few minutes' quiet with an opportunity for individuals to turn to one or two people around them, to chat through the questions and pray for one another. Alternatively, you could tie reflection in to one of the active responses listed in the next section.

Local church story

'Something that we do at the end of some of our youth
services is to get together with others who go to the same
school or hang out in the same environments. We move
from a time of praising God for who he is, to discussing
how we are going to make him known in those contexts.'
Jacob, worship leader, Baptist Church

Ideas to try: making decisions

As well as reflecting, we need to give congregation members
the space to make concrete decisions within a service. People
often find it useful to make physical and symbolic responses.
Sometimes it might be a case of writing something down: the
name of someone you are committing to reach out to on your
frontline, or a fruit of the Spirit you want God to grow in you.
These can be written on paper or something more symbolic:
a salt packet when thinking about Matthew 5:13; or an ID card
if it is a response about our identity being in Christ. Also consider
what people then do with those written commitments: do they
go and place them at the cross, or put them in their wallet or
phone case as a regular reminder, or do they give them to a
friend and ask him or her to pray and keep them accountable?

When you are thinking about the frontlines where the
congregation exists in the week, you might make use of a map
of your local area, and encourage people to place a pin, a Post-it
note or a candle on an area they are committing to. If you are
thinking wider about the UK or other parts of the world, you can
make use of atlases, maps and globes as tactile and visual ways
of committing to places and situations.

Physical posture is another way to enact a decision. Many
churches encourage people to walk to the front or to an area
set aside for prayer. Simply standing up can also be a sign of

commitment. But you may also want to consider other postures – perhaps kneeling is the most appropriate symbol of submission to God in some contexts? Turning towards the door could help symbolize making a commitment to how you will live when you leave the church building. You could have different response stations in different parts of the building, and encourage people to move to the area which best suits their personal response at that moment.

These kinds of responses can be tied in to singing songs of decision, such as 'All to Jesus I Surrender',[4] 'All I Am I Lay It Down'[5] or 'Jesus, You Have Called Us'. This last song is particularly useful as it acknowledges our inadequacy in the things we are committing to:

Jesus, I am willing
though I am weak;
I'll follow you
with your Spirit in me.[6]

This leads us into our third aspect of response.

Receiving from God

Deciding to make a change for God is important, but if we attempt to do it in our own strength we are fooling ourselves. Genuine change comes only from God, as he empowers and transforms us. For this reason, it is important to include moments where the congregation receives from God afresh.

Songs are particularly helpful here because of the way music can open us up emotionally to receive God's Holy Spirit. Paul makes this link in Ephesians 5:18–19: 'be filled with the Spirit by reciting psalms, hymns, and spiritual songs for your own good.'[7] It is not that music has a 'magical' power to summon the Holy Spirit – we should be aware of not attempting to manipulate God or the congregation in this way (see Acts 8:15–23). As Bob Kauflin points out, the swishy sound of a keyboard pad is not the same thing as the Holy Spirit![8] But sensitive use of music and songs can be very helpful in creating the kind of atmosphere where people are open to receiving from God.

Ideas to try: songs for receiving

Simple songs for these moments include 'All Who Are Thirsty',[9] 'Holy Spirit You Are Welcome'[10] and the Taizé chant 'Veni, Sancte Spiritus'.[11] In this context, it is often better to have fewer words and more instrumental space. Singing just the chorus or a few lines can sometimes be more appropriate than ploughing through a whole song.

God is gracious in meeting us with encouragement, love and healing, welcoming us to rest in his presence. Yet his Spirit also empowers us for service: we are blessed to be a blessing. When you want to emphasize this, you may wish to have songs that give some context as to why God is empowering us. The hymn 'Breathe on Me, Breath of God'[12] does this well, as does the Salvation Army hymn 'O God of Burning, Cleansing Flame'.[13] Tim Hughes' song 'Consuming Fire'[14] points to how we are filled up to make a difference in the world, as does the refrain from his song 'God of Justice',[15] which asks God to both fill us up and send us out.

Local church story

'I think there is a danger when worship becomes something that is "done to you" by the person at the front. It becomes a safe spectator activity that doesn't demand a response.

> The more participative our worship becomes, as people are encouraged to interact and engage using their whole selves, the more they are going to take that experience away. We have found having something to take home, which you can see on your way to school or in the kitchen, can bring the response you made on Sunday into normal life.'
> *Eils, curate and worship leader, Church of England*

Commissioning prayer

One further thing we may do in a response time is to commission people. It is typical to hear from, and pray for, people who are going on short-term mission trips, or committing themselves to full-time, paid Christian ministry. However, if we believe that all Christians are 'full-time ministers', that everyone has a mission field on their frontline, and that every act of work, leisure and creativity can be part of building God's kingdom, then should we not be commissioning a much wider variety of people?

Ideas to try: commissioning different groups

Who you commission will depend on the themes of the week and the activities of your church members. But some ideas for commissioning frontline ministers might include the following:

- When a particular industry or issue is in the news, pray for congregation members involved in that area, for example:
  - Around times of elections, get anyone who works in local government and services to stand, and pray for them.
  - When it is exam time, pray for teachers and students.
- Pray for people in different life stages at particular times of the year, perhaps making use of things like Grandparents'

Day, or by making the link with traditional liturgical moments, for example, Rogation Sunday:

– In one Anglican town centre church, the worshippers were asked to arrive dressed as they would ordinarily be dressed for work or daily life, as well as to bring a symbol of their work to place in the offertory. The church leadership explained this approach to the church: 'While traditionally Rogationtide was kept as a time of prayer for the growth and harvest of crops, as ours is not an agricultural congregation we would instead keep the Tide as a time for offering our working lives to God for him to bless the growth of the work we were "planting" in the world.'[16]

– In rural Cambridgeshire we were part of a village church which was built right next to a river. Once a year the church leaders took the Sunday morning service out of doors with the chairs facing the river, and led a service themed around those who work on the waterways. Is there an industry or a profession that your local area is known for? Perhaps you too could annually pray for and commission the people involved in these areas.

• Put regular events in your church diary for frontline commissioning in order to create a balanced church culture. One church in Surrey has established a pattern of running commission events twice a year. The first takes place in the springtime, where the members of the congregation are commissioned for their frontlines, and their life outside the church. The second one, in the autumn, is designed to empower the congregation for its church-based ministries.[17]

• Encourage the members of the congregation to let the church leaders know when they get a new job or role (no matter what sphere, and how big or small it may seem to them). These people can be prayed for as they start to be an influence on their new frontline.

Taking the time to commission different groups of people will help them respond to the call of God on their lives. When we craft careful response times, alert to the Holy Spirit and the needs of our congregation, we can help Sunday's worship continue into the coming week.

---

16. SENDING

Christians are not only called but 'sent': to live lives
which glorify God, to make more disciples of Christ
and to bear witness to God's action in our lives.

Mark Earey[1]

An ending, or a beginning

The final moments of our gathered times of worship have the
potential to provide the key connection with worship on our
frontlines. This moment can make or break the good intentions you had for bridging the gap between gathered and
scattered. Have you ever heard a service end with the following
words?

'Right, well, I guess it might be time for some coffee?'
'OK. That's it. Goodbye.'
'You are dismissed.'

If worship is thought of as a journey, then the words above
represent crashing into a brick wall!

A more sensitive leader might say: 'This is the end of our
time of worship. See you next week when we'll worship

again', but once more we are asked to park our worship there and then. Instead, we need to provide signposts, directing the worshippers through this particular junction, to help transition from 'gathered' to 'scattered'. As Clayton Schmit points out:

> The sending forth of gathered worshippers is the pivotal moment when worship turns from adoration to action . . . In this final moment of worship, the gathered become the sent. They are not dismissed as if worship were adjourned.[2]

In the last blessing, closing words or final song, the worship leader or planner has the opportunity to set the agenda for the week ahead. We could give the impression that Monday to Saturday are wasted days, which God cares little about. Or we could show that God cares deeply. We can dismiss the congregation in such a way as to imply that, because people do not work full time as pastors and evangelists, they are going out into meaningless drudgery. Or we could send out everyone – full-time mums, lawyers, checkout assistants and more – into the world with a mission and a purpose. Does worship have to end with the final ringing of the strummed chord? Or can it seamlessly continue into our lives of obedience?

We should be helping the members of our congregations continue in what Matt Redman calls 'Unbroken Praise',[3] living an entire life surrendered to God, where our deeds 'outrun' our words, and our lives 'outweigh' our songs.

Purposeful words

The words we use at the end of a service have the potential to make a great impact, provided we choose well and put some care into planning them. Traditionally, a church worship service will end with what is known as a 'Benediction', which comes from Latin, meaning 'to speak a good word'.[4] What 'good words' or blessings could you speak over your congregation? There are biblical blessings, such as Aaron's blessing from Numbers 6, and several examples of Jesus praying to send out his followers in the Gospels.[5] Constance Cherry points out, however, that Jesus does not bless without also adding a 'charge', or a challenge, and that we must learn from this too: 'A blessing without a charge lacks the connection to service; a charge without a blessing lacks the sense of power needed for service.'[6]

The congregation members need to know that as they leave, the presence of God goes with them: 'And surely I am with you always' (Matthew 28:20); but they also need to know that they are leaving the sanctuary with a mission: 'As the Father has sent me, I am sending you' (John 20:21). Traditional liturgical words such as 'Go in peace to love and serve the Lord / In the name of Christ. Amen' also serve very well here. As Mark Earey puts it: 'Our sending is more than being blessed; our sending is taking the blessing with us.'[7]

Ideas to try: prayers for sending

Look for written prayers that emphasize this kind of sending, like this one from the Iona Community:

> From where we are
> to where you need us,
> Jesus, now lead on.
> From the security of what we know
> to the adventure of what you will reveal,
> Jesus, now lead on.
> To refashion the fabric of this world
> until it resembles the shape of your kingdom,
> Jesus, now lead on.

Because good things have been prepared
for those who love God,
Jesus, now lead on.[8]

Paul's letters in the New Testament also provide good inspiration
for blessings to speak over the church (e.g. Romans 15:13, 33;
2 Corinthians 13:11–14). One example of how you can adapt
a Bible passage into words of blessing comes from Philippians
1:3–11:

May you find joy in each other.
May you find gospel partnerships in each other.
May he who began a good work in you
carry it on to completion until the day of Christ Jesus.

May you carry each other in your hearts,
and share God's grace with each other.
May you have the affection of Jesus Christ for each other.

May your love abound more and more,
in knowledge and depth of insight,
so that you may be able to discern what is best
and may be pure and blameless for the day of Christ,
filled with the fruit of righteousness that comes through
Jesus Christ –
to the glory and praise of God.
Amen.[9]

We also encourage you to write your own 'good words', suitable
for your specific context.

Written words can be as powerful as spoken ones; for example,
we heard of someone who removed the sign saying 'You are now
entering a place of worship' from the outside of their church door.
Instead, they hung it on the inside of the doorway. When the

worshippers left the building, the sign reminded them that the sphere they were entering as they left the sanctuary was, in fact, a place where worship could continue.

Songs

Many churches leave it to the sung worship leader to decide the final words of the service. Some songs might imply that worship is coming to an end. But here is a chance to help the members of the congregation commit to continue worshipping God as they leave the building.

Ideas to try: singing your sending

There are hymn texts that help with this: 'Forth in Your Name',[10] 'Father, Help Your People'[11] or 'Be the God of All My Sundays':

> Be the God of all my Sundays,
> be the focus of my praise;
> it is you I choose to honour
> on this special day of days.
> God who made me, God who saved me,
> with your people I belong
> as we come to hear you speaking
> and to join our hearts in song.
>
> Be the God of all my Mondays:
> let my lifestyle make you known;
> give me courage in confession
> when for you I stand alone.
> Be my God through work and leisure,
> rest and travel, day and night;
> let me keep a clear awareness
> of a life lived in your sight.

Be the God I serve and worship
day by day, throughout the week,
God whose flawless care sustains me,
God whose guiding word I seek.
Be my God through every moment,
every circumstance I face,
God of life in its completeness,
God of holy, daily grace.[12]

We also regularly use the well-known song 'I Will Worship',[13]
but sing it at the end of the service rather than at the start.
This changes the meaning from an intention about the gathered
worship to instead point towards our scattered worship. How will
we worship God with our hearts, souls, minds and strength out
on our frontlines? We have used pictures of everyday activities,
such as washing up, mowing the lawn, having a cup of coffee and
so on, as backgrounds behind the words. Singing words that tell
God we will bow down and give him everything over a picture of
someone handling a credit card, or sitting at a desk, can help us
commit to worshipful responses in our daily lives.

Ideas to try: 'Just do it'

A final idea is an interactive declaration, based on Romans 12.[14]
Explain that when the leader says 'Just do it', the congregation is
to respond: 'This is our worship.'

[*Leader*] So here's what I want you to do, God helping you:
          Take your everyday, ordinary life
          – your sleeping, eating, going-to-work and walking-
          around life –
          and place it before God as an offering.
          Just do it:
[*All*]   **this is our worship.**

In Christ we, though many, form one body, and each
member belongs to all the others. We all have different
gifts.
If it's prophesying – just do it:
this is our worship.
If it's serving – just do it:
this is our worship.
If it's teaching – just do it:
this is our worship.
If it's encouraging – just do it:
this is our worship.
If it's giving – just do it:
this is our worship.
If it's leading – just do it:
this is our worship.
If it's showing mercy – just do it:
this is our worship.
Love must be sincere. Hate what's evil; cling to
what's good.
Be joyful in hope, patient in trouble, faithful in
prayer.
Be generous and invite people around.
Just do it:
this is our worship.
Don't hit back, but show love. Care for each other,
be a friend to those who are alone.
Don't take revenge; if a bully is hungry and thirsty,
give him food and drink.
Just do it:
this is our worship.

We then invite people to share what they do in their everyday
life, for example, 'I'm a bank manager', 'I go to school', 'I care for

my sister'. After each phrase, use the response: 'Just do it: This is our worship.'

Finally, in order to make the 'sending' physical, it can be helpful to avoid a situation where people slump back into their chairs after they've been 'sent'. You can encourage them to stay standing up and start moving – it might only be to the coffee area, but it's a start! That way, they are more clearly obeying the challenge to go and get on with worship on their frontlines. Songs, prayers, words and actions like this will gradually shift your church culture to seeing the whole of life as a grateful response of worship to the God who calls and sends us.

17. FIRST STEPS FORWARD

You will have understood by now that we are not promoting a superficial fad or stylistic tweak in worship, but a deep culture shift to include all three dimensions within church services, drawing from and inspiring people towards whole lives of scattered worship. We hope that you will make full use of the many ideas and concepts we have presented, and that you are feeling challenged and equipped. But we also pray that you will not feel overwhelmed – we know that this can sometimes be a reality when faced with bringing change to a church culture. To help you with this, here are some first steps for moving forward. We would also encourage you to take a look at the *Whole Life Worship: Journey Pack*, which includes five service plans, sermon outlines, usable worship resources, and song and hymn suggestions, all designed to help your church continue on this journey.[1]

Evolution, not revolution

The first thing to say is that this transformation cannot happen fully and significantly overnight, or even in a few weeks or months. Genuine culture change takes years. But it can happen if we follow the principle of the 'one-degree shift'. A small, almost imperceptible movement like one degree of a compass can make a big difference over time. Neil Hudson explains that these changes 'are not meant to be spectacular transformations, merely part of a long-term process that will lead to a more profound shift in emphasis'.[2]

Jacqueline, an Anglican lay reader, told us of how one activity bore fruit when her church persisted with it:

> We did an activity to help us engage outwards: A3 sheets of paper were put all around the walls, with different categories such as 'office worker', 'home-maker', 'education' etc. I remember the first time we did it, people were a bit like 'What is this?' in that muttering kind of way. When they gathered at their station, all they had to do was pray for each other, but they were quite reluctant. Yet over time their openness grew, and we found that people then started to pray for one another during the week. People didn't know that, for example, someone fostered, or looked after a relative with dementia. All these kinds of stories came out, and it engaged people and they began to bless each other.
>
> One of the most successful groups was the office workers. They were very reluctant to share prayer needs, tending to be the ones who wouldn't naturally speak out. But as they began to share, they discovered that many of them often felt compromised as Christians in the office environment. There was a vulnerability within them that only got healed within

that like-minded group, over time. That was the effect of this quite simple prayer exercise, which gave deep roots for people and a connectedness.

Low-hanging fruit

Another image is of a tree with many ripe apples ready for harvest, but most of these will require a ladder to reach. What do you do first? You start by reaching up and grabbing the lowest-hanging fruit. These represent the easier 'one-degree shifts' for your context. So for example, some churches already pray intercessory prayers every week. It might be a low-hanging fruit to turn the subject of these outward, towards people's frontlines. You might be used to learning new songs, so adding some with a whole-life emphasis will be straightforward. If your All Age services are already creative, it may be simple to include a creative prayer activity for your local area. Which are the low-hanging fruit in your context?

Do it in a team

It is almost impossible to make any significant change on your own. If you are a pastor or person responsible for worship, you will need to bring your teams on board to develop worship culture in this area. You will also need to get the perspectives of team members, and draw from their gifts and spheres of influence.

Perhaps begin with a few one-to-one conversations with key leaders. Who would be an important ally in this change: creative people, musicians, writers, small-group leaders, children's and youth ministers? You could share this book with them or make use of our accompanying *Whole Life Worship:*

Journey Pack.[3] Then begin to widen the team, encouraging and supporting one another each time you experiment with a fresh form of gathered worship.

If you are not the church leader or person responsible for worship, you may find it harder to build a team or get your leaders' buy-in. There may be areas of church services that you have no influence over. In this case, do what you can to share your heart for this issue with those in authority. But the reality may be that you need to begin with what is in your sphere of influence. Which are the low-hanging fruit for you? How can you demonstrate, within the opportunities you do have, how gathered worship can look outward?

Mix understanding with experiences

Some people will 'get' this when you explain it to them – using this book, our *Journey Pack*, or teaching it from the Bible in sermons or small groups. However, many others will need to experience it. Blend understanding with opportunities to actually worship in this way. Make use of the ideas we have given in this book. Anita, a discipleship and families worker, has shared an idea her church used:

> To help people connect what they do on a Sunday to their scattered lives, sometimes we've found it is helpful to actually get out of the building during church worship. So at the end of the service we have broken up for a choice of activities – some people going on a prayer walk, others going into the school field, others doing a craft activity. It has helped to be out in the real world during the worship, among other people doing different things on a Sunday morning. I think that has really enriched the idea that worship is for every day.

Sometimes your teaching will take the form of 'back-reflecting', as you say something like: 'Remember when we prayed for our local businesses? That was an example of our worship engaging with the third dimension.'

Have grace to make mistakes

The heart of the gospel is forgiveness and restoration. So make this the case for the way you and your team lead worship. Be prepared to take a risk, to not get something quite right, and to know God's grace in your efforts. Talk about what has gone well, and how you can improve things in the future. In this way, you will step out of your comfort zones and begin to grow. Together, you will learn to lead worship that engages a fuller picture of God and a greater participation of his people, empowering them to go out and live their whole lives for his glory.

We will close with a prayer we often use to begin services, encouraging congregation members to bring their whole selves to worship. Join us in praying it now, and know that God is sending you out to worship him with your whole life:

[*Leader*] Come to worship!
Come and give God all you are!
Put your hearts into it: make up your minds
to give him the best.

[*All*]   **With all our hearts we worship.**

Open up your souls and spirits –
let his Spirit move and touch you.
With all our souls we worship.

Don't switch off your brains:
worship him thoughtfully and intelligently.
With all our minds we worship.

Put your back into it:
never tire of exalting God and showing others
you mean it.
With all our strength we worship.

All creation gives glory to God:
everything I am comes to give him the best I can.
Amen![4]

APPENDIX 1: TOP CCLI WORSHIP SONGS

Below is the list of songs we analysed in chapter 6, as of September 2015.

UK Christian Copyright Licensing International top twenty-five

1. 'In Christ Alone', Keith Getty, Stuart Townend
2. 'Be Still', David J. Evans
3. 'Here I Am to Worship', Tim Hughes
4. 'Psalm 23', Stuart Townend
5. 'Shout to the Lord', Darlene Zschech
6. 'How Deep the Father's Love for Us', Stuart Townend
7. 'How Great Is Our God', Ed Cash, Jesse Reeves, Chris Tomlin
8. 'How Great Thou Art', Stuart Wesley Keene Hine
9. 'King of Kings, Majesty', Jarrod Cooper
10. '10,000 Reasons (Bless the Lord)', Jonas Myrin, Matt Redman
11. 'There Is a Redeemer', Melody Green
12. 'Blessed Be Your Name', Beth Redman, Matt Redman

13. 'The Servant King', Graham Kendrick
14. 'Shine Jesus Shine', Graham Kendrick
15. 'Great Is Thy Faithfulness', Thomas Obediah Chisholm
16. 'Faithful One', Brian Doerksen
17. 'Come, Now Is the Time to Worship', Brian Doerksen
18. 'I Will Offer Up My Life', Matt Redman
19. 'Everlasting God', Brenton Brown, Ken Riley
20. 'Knowing You', Graham Kendrick
21. 'Mighty to Save', Ben Fielding, Reuben Morgan
22. 'All Heaven Declares', Noel Richards, Tricia Richards
23. 'Lord, I Lift Your Name on High', Rick Founds
24. 'Forever', Chris Tomlin
25. 'Hosanna (Praise Is Rising)', Paul Baloche, Brenton Brown

USA Christian Copyright Licensing International top twenty-five

1. '10,000 Reasons (Bless the Lord)', Jonas Myrin, Matt Redman
2. 'This Is Amazing Grace', Jeremy Riddle, Josh Farro, Phil Wickham
3. 'Cornerstone', Edward Mote, Eric Liljero, Jonas Myrin, Reuben Morgan, William Batchelder Bradbury
4. 'Oceans (Where Feet May Fail)', Joel Houston, Matt Crocker, Salomon Ligthelm
5. 'Lord, I Need You', Christy Nockels, Daniel Carson, Jesse Reeves, Kristian Stanfill, Matt Maher
6. 'One Thing Remains (Your Love Never Fails)', Brian Johnson, Christa Black Gifford, Jeremy Riddle
7. 'Our God', Chris Tomlin, Jesse Reeves, Jonas Myrin, Matt Redman
8. 'How Great Is Our God', Chris Tomlin, Ed Cash, Jesse Reeves

9. 'Forever Reign', Jason Ingram, Reuben Morgan
10. 'Mighty to Save', Ben Fielding, Reuben Morgan
11. 'In Christ Alone', Keith Getty, Stuart Townend
12. 'Amazing Grace (My Chains Are Gone)', Chris Tomlin, John Newton, Louie Giglio
13. 'Revelation Song', Jennie Lee Riddle
14. 'Holy Spirit', Bryan Torwalt, Katie Torwalt
15. 'Here I Am to Worship', Tim Hughes
16. 'Blessed Be Your Name', Beth Redman, Matt Redman
17. 'How He Loves', John Mark McMillan
18. 'The Stand', Joel Houston
19. 'This I Believe (The Creed)', Ben Fielding, Matt Crocker
20. 'Whom Shall I Fear (God of Angel Armies)', Chris Tomlin, Ed Cash, Scott Cash
21. 'Everlasting God', Brenton Brown, Ken Riley
22. 'Open Up the Heavens', Andi Rozier, James McDonald, Jason Ingram, Meredith Andrews, Stuart Garrard
23. 'Alive', Alexander Pappas, Aodhan King
24. 'Forever (We Sing Hallelujah)', Brian Johnson, Christa Black Gifford, Gabriel Wilson, Jenn Johnson, Joel Taylor, Kari Jobe
25. 'Jesus Messiah', Chris Tomlin, Daniel Carson, Ed Cash, Jesse Reeves

APPENDIX 2: SMALL-GROUP DISCUSSION IN CHURCH

There are sometimes issues surrounding getting people to talk in pairs or small groups within a church service. For some people this is a great opportunity to share perspectives and questions. It engages the 'horizontal' dynamic, breaking out of the 'me and God and forget the world' dualism. It can help people root the worship and teaching within their frontline experiences.

However, for others there may be a natural reluctance, shyness or even fear of being asked to talk to a neighbour in church. So here are a few pointers that we try to follow:

- Make your questions open-ended and more about people's opinions or experiences, rather than expecting them to come up with a 'correct' answer. For example: 'Are there situations in the news or the world which have caught your attention recently?' 'Are there aspects of prayer that you struggle with?' 'Where in your week might you have an opportunity to shine God's light?' Avoid: 'What does this text mean?' 'How often do you pray?' 'Share your biggest sin with the stranger next to you.'

- Invite and encourage; don't demand. When you invite people to get into groups (or do anything in church), give a get-out: 'You might want to turn to the person next to you and discuss . . . but if you just want to sit quietly that is fine too.' You can add the option to write answers on a piece of paper and hand them back or, if you are technologically capable, people could text or tweet a response.
- Explain the question clearly and concisely (have it written in front of you), and then have it repeated on a projection screen or handout.
- Limit the time of discussion, and let people know: 'We are going to talk about this for three minutes, and then we will sing again.' In this way, conversations are kept concise and people who are squirming in their seat can see light at the end of the tunnel!

APPENDIX 3: USING DIGITAL IMAGES

Many churches benefit from having projectors or flat-screen monitors. However, few have really grasped the full potential for enhancing the visual aspect of worship for congregations. It is easy to either underuse the technology, or go overboard and end up with something distracting. Here are a few tips to get you started:

- Do less with greater quality. For example, choose one fairly plain but attractive background as the default for all your worship songs and texts. Then experiment with using more creative images for, say, just one song or prayer per service, to get you started.
- Make sure your images are of a high enough resolution for your screen. Even the most basic projector is 800 × 600 pixels (and many are higher). If your image is, say, 300 × 180 it will end up pixelated if you drag it to the full screen. Also beware of stretching images out of proportion (check if your projector is operating at the standard 4:3 ratio or widescreen 16:9 ratio).

- If you're trying to set words over images, there are
  a few ways you can keep the text legible:
  - use areas of a single colour, with minimal details or
    contrast, to put the text over;
  - use an outline and/or a glow on the text to make it
    stand out (white text with a black border is usually
    the most legible);
  - create a semi-transparent dark box, which still shows
    some of the image, but will make white text stand out.
- Be sure to check readability on the actual screen because
  it may look very different from how your home
  computer displays it.
- Also be aware of people with visual impairment or
  Specific Learning Difficulties (such as dyslexia or
  dyspraxia), who may need special consideration such as
  creating a large-print version of all the text as a handout.
  Have conversations with people who have such needs,
  or their carers, and determine what will be most
  appropriate.
- Be aware of copyright issues associated with using other
  people's images. Rather than just Google searching, try
  some of the great websites that offer pictures for free
  or with a Creative Commons licence: <unsplash.com>,
  <freeimages.com>, <splitshire.com>, <lifeofpix.com>,
  <gratisography.com> and more.
- Even better – create images yourself, and/or encourage
  your congregation to do the same. You could have an
  online database where anyone in church can submit
  photos or graphics, which you could then choose from.
  Or ask a talented photographer or designer to come up
  with a selection of images on a theme. We talk about
  'crowdsourcing' images for intercession in chapter 10.

NOTES

1. Worship and the frontline

1. Matt Redman, 'Matt Redman Is Facedown', *Relevant* (April 2004), <http://www.relevantmagazine.com/god/worship/features/607-matt-redman-is-facedown>.
2. David Ruis, © 1991 Shade Tree Music (Admin. by Song Solutions), Universal Music – Brentwood Benson Publishing (Admin. by Song Solutions). We describe this idea further in ch. 16, p. 150.
3. Andy Mitchell, in correspondence with the authors, May 2016.
4. Quoted in Neil Hudson, *Imagine Church: Releasing Whole-Life Disciples* (IVP, 2012), p. 31.
5. Mark Greene, *The Great Divide* (LICC, 2010), p. 13.
6. Basil the Great, *Homilia in psalmum I*, quoted in John Witvliet, *The Biblical Psalms in Christian Worship: Brief Introduction and Guide to Resources* (Eerdmans, 2007), p. 4.
7. Quoted in Barry Liesch, *The New Worship: Straight Talk on Music and the Church* (Baker, 2001), p. 51.

8. Graham Cray, 'Justice, Rock and the Renewal of Worship', in Robin Sheldon (ed.), *In Spirit and in Truth: Exploring Directions in Music in Worship Today* (Hodder and Stoughton, 1989), p. 11.

9. Hudson, *Imagine Church*, p. 30.

10. Mark Greene, *Fruitfulness on the Frontline: Making a Difference Where You Are* (IVP, 2014).

11. John Witvliet, 'The Cumulative Power of Transformation in Public Worship', in Alexis D. Abernethy (ed.), *Worship that Changes Lives: Multidisciplinary and Congregational Perspectives on Spiritual Transformation* (Baker Academic, 2008), p. 44.

12. John Witvliet, 'Soul Food for the People of God', in *Worship Seeking Understanding* (Baker Academic, 2003), pp. 231–249.

13. Witvliet, 'Cumulative Power', pp. 50–51.

14. Simon Foster, *What Helps Disciples Grow?* (St Peter's Saltley Trust, 2016), <www.saltleytrust.org.uk/whdg>.

15. Foster, *What Helps*, p. 18.

16. Please note: we have intentionally not included preaching as a topic. We do see sermons and teaching as an absolutely key part of worship services. However, we do not feel we could do the topic justice within the confines of this book; preaching for the frontline deserves a book all of its own.

2. All of life can be worship

1. Abraham Kuyper, quoted in Harry Boonstra (ed.), *Abraham Kuyper: Our Worship* (Eerdmans, 2009), p. 18.

2. Mark Greene, *Fruitfulness on the Frontline: Making a Difference Where You Are* (IVP, 2014), p. 36.

3. Rick Warren, *The Purpose-Driven Life: What on Earth Am I Here For?* (Zondervan, 2002), pp. 66–67.

4. David Peterson, *Engaging with God: A Biblical Theology of Worship* (Apollos, 1992), p. 18, emphasis ours.

5. Peterson, *Engaging*, p. 97.

6. Miroslav Volf, 'Worship as Adoration and Action: Reflections on a Christian Way of Being in the World', in D. A. Carson (ed.), *Worship: Adoration and Action* (Paternoster Press, 1993), p. 204.

7. Andrew Hill, *Enter His Courts with Praise* (Kingsway, 1998), pp. 141–142.

8. Peterson, *Engaging*, p. 64.

9. Colin G. Kruse, *Paul's Letter to the Romans* (Apollos, 2012), p. 462.

10. F. F. Bruce, New International Commentary on the New Testament, *The Epistles to the Colossians, to Philemon, and to the Ephesians* (Eerdmans, 1984), p. 160.

11. John Calvin, quoted in Kruse, *Paul's Letter*, p. 461.

12. The phrase 'in your hearts' does not imply silent or simply inward worship, but rather 'is employed to refer to the whole of one's being'. A better translation might be 'from your hearts'. Peter T. O'Brien, Word Biblical Commentary, *Colossians–Philemon* (Word, 1982), p. 210.

13. Notice that as in Hebrews, we are not worshipping in our own strength. It is in the name of Jesus and through him that we are able to give thanks to our Father.

14. Ralph P. Martin, *Colossians: The Church's Lord and the Christian's Liberty* (Paternoster Press, 1972), pp. 127–128.

15. David Kinnaman, 'Six Reasons Young People Leave the Church', <http://www.christianitytoday.com/le/2012/winter/youngleavechurch.html>.

3. Does gathered worship matter?

1. Stuart Murray, *Church After Christendom* (Authentic, 2005), p. 205.

2. Gerard Kelly, *Church Actually: Rediscovering the Brilliance of God's Plan* (Monarch, 2011), p. 23.

3. The dots illustration is a method LICC have used for a number of years to illustrate gathered and scattered discipleship.

4. Abraham Kuyper, 'Sphere Sovereignty', in James Bratt (ed.), *Abraham Kuyper: A Centennial Reader* (Eerdmans, 1998), p. 448.

5. Abraham Kuyper, quoted in Harry Boonstra (ed.), *Abraham Kuyper: Our Worship* (Eerdmans, 2009), p. 18.

6. Quoted in James F. White, *A Brief History of Christian Worship* (Abingdon Press, 1993), p. 31.

7. David Peterson, *Engaging with God: A Biblical Theology of Worship* (Apollos, 1992), p. 202.

8. Eugene Peterson, *Leap Over A Wall: Earthy Spirituality for Everyday Christians* (HarperSanFrancisco, 1997), pp. 152–153, quoted in Alan Kreider and Eleanor Kreider, *Worship and Mission after Christendom* (Paternoster Press, 2009), p. 10.

9. Graham Cray, interview with authors, 15 January 2016.

10. Miroslav Volf, 'Worship as Adoration and Action: Reflections on a Christian Way of Being in the World', in D. A. Carson (ed.), *Worship: Adoration and Action* (Paternoster Press, 1993), p. 211.

4. Is your worship 3D?

1. Mark Earey, *Liturgical Worship: A Fresh Look* (Church House Publishing, 2009), p. 14.

2. See Bob Hopkins, Mike Breen, *Clusters: Creative Mid-Sized Missional Communities* (3DM, 2007), p. 60. You can also read about three-dimensional church in the Mission Shaped Church report: Graham Cray et al., *Mission Shaped Church* (Church House Publishing, 2004), pp. 96–99.

3. Frost and Hirsch use the terminology of three relationships: communion (in relationship with Christ, including the sub-feature 'worship'), community (relationship with one another) and commission (relationship with the world).

Michael Frost and Alan Hirsch, *The Shaping of Things to Come: Innovation and Mission for the 21st-Century Church* (Hendrickson, 2003), pp. 78–79.

4. Ralph P. Martin, *The Worship of God: Some Theological, Pastoral and Practical Reflections* (Eerdmans, 1994), p. 10.

5. There is always the chance someone could read a passage like Psalm 137:9, but it hasn't happened to us yet . . .

6. © Joel Payne / <RESOUNDworship.org>, administered by The Jubilate Group. <www.resoundworship.org/song/hes_my_saviour>.

7. © Geraldine Latty / <RESOUNDworship.org>, administered by The Jubilate Group, <www.jubilate.co.uk>. Used by permission. <www.resoundworship.org/song/lord_you_hear_the_cry_lord_have_mercy>.

8. Stuart Townend, Simon Brading, copyright © 2011 Thankyou Music (Adm. by <CapitolCMGPublishing.com> excl. UK & Europe, adm. by Integrity Music, part of the David C. Cook family, <songs@integritymusic.com>), used by permission.

9. <www.stuarttownend.co.uk/song/christ-be-in-my-waking/>.

5. New journeys of worship

1. Andy Flannagan, *Distinctive Worship: How A New Generation Connects with God* (Authentic, 2004), p. 19.

2. David Peterson, *Engaging with God: A Biblical Theology of Worship* (Apollos, 1992), p. 67.

3. Alan Kreider and Eleanor Kreider, *Worship and Mission after Christendom* (Paternoster Press, 2009), p. 5. Also Mark Earey, *Liturgical Worship: A Fresh Look* (Church House Publishing, 2009), pp. 14–15.

4. Constance M. Cherry, *The Worship Architect: A Blueprint for Designing Culturally Relevant and Biblically Faithful Services* (Baker, 2010), pp. 35–122.

5. This model is our edited version; Cherry makes many more suggestions.

6. James F. White, *Protestant Worship: Traditions in Transition* (Westminster John Knox Press, 1989), pp. 171–191.

7. Ralph P. Martin, *The Worship of God: Some Theological, Pastoral and Practical Reflections* (Eerdmans, 1994), p. 9.

8. See Barry Liesch, *The New Worship: Straight Talk on Music and the Church* (Baker, 2001), p. 55. For another variation which puts 'intimacy' fourth and the 'giving of substance' fifth, see John Wimber, 'Why We Worship and the Phases of Worship', *Equipping the Saints*, vol. 1, no. 1, available at <http:// trinityvf.org/wordpress/index.php/2012/12/why-we-worship-the-phases-of-worship-by-john-wimber>.

9. Gary Thomas has identified nine spiritual temperaments, different 'pathways' through which people most naturally and appropriately connect with God. These include traditionalists, activists, contemplatives and enthusiasts – each preferring different but equally valid styles of worship. Gary Thomas, *Sacred Pathways: Discover Your Soul's Path to God* (Zondervan, 2000).

10. This idea comes from Bob Rognlien, *Experiential Worship: Encountering God with Heart, Soul, Mind and Strength* (Navpress, 2005). The table is our adapted version of his on p. 22.

6. The language of songs

1. Graham Cray, 'Justice, Rock and the Renewal of Worship', in Robin Sheldon (ed.), *In Spirit and in Truth: Exploring Directions in Music in Worship Today* (Hodder and Stoughton, 1989), p. 19.

2. Nick Page, *And Now Let's Move into a Time of Nonsense: Why Worship Songs Are Failing the Church* (Authentic, 2004), p. 99.

3. Page, *And Now Let's*, p. 26.

4. Sue Rinaldi, interview, 22 February 2016.

5. Tom Wright, *Surprised by Hope* (SPCK, 2007), p. 102.

6. Cray, 'Justice, Rock', p. 4.

7. Full lists of songs analysed can be found in appendix 1.

8. Christopher J. Voke, *Creation at Worship: Ecology, Creation and Christian Worship* (Paternoster Press, 2009), p. 52.

9. See Robert E. Webber, *Who Gets to Narrate the World?: Contending for the Christian Story in an Age of Rivals* (IVP, 2008), p. 29.

10. 'How Great Thou Art', © 1949 and 1953 Stuart K. Hine Trust (Admin. by Integrity Music).

11. 'This I Believe' by Ben Fielding, Matt Crocker, © 2014 Hillsong Music Publishing (Admin. by Capitol CMG Publishing).

12. 'The Stand', words and music by Joel Houston, © 2005 Hillsong Music Publishing (APRA). CCLI: 4705248, used by permission.

13. 'Great Is Thy Faithfulness' by Thomas Chisholm, © 1923. Renewed 1951 Hope Publishing Company. This is also reflected in the chorus of 'Shout to the Lord' by Darlene Zschech, © 1993 Wondrous Worship (Admin. by Song Solutions <www.songsolutions.org>).

14. 'Revelation Song' by Jennie Lee Riddle, © 2004 Gateway Create Publishing (Admin. by Capitol CMG Publishing (IMI)).

15. Pete Ward, *Growing Up Evangelical: The Making of a Subculture* (SPCK, 1996), p. 136.

16. 'Open Up the Heavens' by Andi Rozier, James McDonald, Jason Ingram, Meredith Andrews, Stuart Garrard, © 2012 Word Music, LLC (a div. of Word Music Group, Inc.), HBC Worship Music (Admin. by Essential Music Publishing LLC), Open Hands Music (Admin. by Essential Music Publishing LLC), Studio Music Publishing (Admin. by Essential Music Publishing LLC), Sony/ATV Timber Publishing (Admin. by Sony/ATV Music Publishing).

17. Voke, *Creation at Worship*, p. 69.

18. 'God in Such Love for Us Lent Us This Planet' by Fred Pratt Green, © 1973 Stainer & Bell Ltd, 23 Gruneisen Road, London, N3 1DZ, England, <www.stainer.co.uk>, used with permission.

19. 'In Christ Alone' by Keith Getty, Stuart Townend, © 2001 Thankyou Music (Admin. by Integrity Music); 'This I Believe' by Ben Fielding, Matt Crocker; 'Lord, I Lift Your Name on High' by Rich Founds, © 1989 Universal Music – Brentwood Benson Publishing (Admin. by Song Solutions <www. songsolutions.org>); 'Here I Am to Worship' by Tim Hughes, © 2000 Thankyou Music (Admin. by Integrity Music); 'The Servant King' by Graham Kendrick, © 1983 Thankyou Music, <www.grahamkendrick.co.uk/songs/item/23-the-servant-king-from-heaven-you-came>.

20. Ward, *Growing Up*, pp. 116–117.

21. 'Oceans (Where Feet May Fail)' by Joel Houston, Matt Crocker, Salomon Ligthelm, © 2012 Hillsong Music Publishing (Admin. by Capitol CMG Publishing).

22. 'All the Room Was Hushed and Still' by Graham Kendrick, © 2009 Make Way Music, based on the foot-washing story from John 13.

23. 'The Summons (Will You Come and Follow Me)' by John L. Bell, © 1987, Iona Community, GIA Publications, Inc., based on the calling of the disciples and other snapshots from Jesus' life.

24. 'The Stand', words and music by Joel Houston, © 2005 Hillsong Music Publishing (APRA). CCLI: 4705248, used by permission. Emphasis ours.

25. 'Shine Jesus Shine' by Graham Kendrick, © 1987 Make Way Music (Admin. by Music Services, Inc.).

26. © Sam Hargreaves / <RESOUNDworship.org>, administered by The Jubilate Group, <www.jubilate.co.uk>. Used by permission. <www.resoundworship.org/song/christ_was_raised>.

27. Wright, *Surprised*, p. 37; for a fuller unpacking of
     1 Corinthians 15, see pp. 165–169.

28. Voke, *Creation at Worship*, p. 71.

29. 'There Is a Redeemer' by Melody Green, © 1982 Birdwing
     Music / Ears To Hear Music / Universal Music – Brentwood
     Benson Publishing (Adm. <CapitolCMGPublishing.com> /
     UK&Eire Song Solutions <www.songsolutions.org>). All
     rights reserved. Used by permission.

30. Wright, *Surprised*, pp. 29–30. Both Wright and Sara (who happens
     to be Swedish) like to point out that the original Swedish version
     of this hymn has much better theology in its final verse!

31. 'Amazing Grace (My Chains Are Gone)' by Chris Tomlin,
     John Newton, Louie Giglio, © 2006 sixsteps Music (Admin.
     by Integrity Music).

32. Wade Burleson, 'Better to Get Theology from Scripture,
     not Songs', <www.wadeburleson.org/2009/06/better-to-get-
     theology-from-scripture.html>.

33. 'On That Day' by Geraldine Latty, © 2007 Thankyou Music
     (Adm. by <CapitolCMGPublishing.com> excl. UK & Europe,
     adm. by Integrity Music, part of the David C. Cook family,
     <songs@integritymusic.com>). Used with permission.

7. Gathering

1. Michael W. Goheen, 'Nourishing Our Missional Identity:
    Worship and the Mission of God's People', in David J. Cohen
    and Michael Parsons (eds.), *In Praise of Worship: An Exploration
    of Text and Practice* (Wipf and Stock, 2010), p. 51.

2. Clayton J. Schmit, *Sent and Gathered: A Worship Manual for the
    Missional Church* (Baker Academic, 2009), p. 161.

3. Constance M. Cherry, *The Worship Architect: A Blueprint for
    Designing Culturally Relevant and Biblically Faithful Services*
    (Baker, 2010), p. 38.

4. Cherry, *The Worship Architect*, p. 54.
5. Keith Getty, Kristyn Getty, Stuart Townend, © 2007 Thankyou Music (Admin. by Integrity Music).
6. © Mark Earey. Used by permission. Available with PowerPoint slides on <engageworship.org/WholeLifeResources>.
7. Schmit, *Sent and Gathered*, p. 162.
8. <engageworship.org/WholeLifeResources>.
9. © Sam Hargreaves / <RESOUNDworship.org>, administered by The Jubilate Group, <www.jubilate.co.uk>. Used by permission. <www.resoundworship.org/song/come_you_thankful_people>.
10. Download the PowerPoint slides from <engageworship.org/WholeLifeResources>.
11. Matt and Beth Redman, © 2002 Kingsway's Thankyou Music.
12. Schmit, *Sent and Gathered*, p. 168.
13. © Bob Hartman. Used by permission.
14. © Joel Payne / <RESOUNDworship.org>, administered by The Jubilate Group, <www.jubilate.co.uk>. Used by permission. <www.resoundworship.org/song/as_we_gather_whatever_we_do>.

8. Praise

1. J. G. Davies, *Worship and Mission* (SCM Press, 1966), p. 119.
2. Henry Francis Lyte, public domain.
3. Jesse Reeves, Matt Maher, Matt Redman, Tim Wanstall, © 2011 Chrysalis Music Ltd. (Admin. by BMG Chrysalis US), sixsteps Music (Admin. by Integrity Music), Thankyou Music (Admin. by Integrity Music), Valley Of Songs Music (Admin. by Integrity Music), <worshiptogether.com> songs (Admin. by Integrity Music).
4. Public domain.

5. For a creative and energetic paraphrase of Psalm 96, see Bob Hartman's version here: <engageworship.org/WholeLifeResources>.

6. This reading of the Psalms comes from Michael W. Goheen, 'Nourishing Our Missional Identity: Worship and the Mission of God's People', in David J. Cohen and Michael Parsons (eds.), *In Praise of Worship: An Exploration of Text and Practice* (Wipf and Stock, 2010), pp. 40–48.

7. We have created a visually engaging PowerPoint with Psalm 67, interspersed with prayers of praise and intercession: <engageworship.org/WholeLifeResources>.

8. John Witvliet, *The Biblical Psalms in Christian Worship: Brief Introduction and Guide to Resources* (Eerdmans, 2007), p. 20.

9. Alan Kreider and Eleanor Kreider, *Worship and Mission after Christendom* (Paternoster Press, 2009), p. 137.

10. <www.churchofengland.org/prayer-worship/worship/texts/daily2/canticles/othercanticles.aspx>.

11. Catherine Winkworth, Joachim Neander, public domain. These slightly modernized lyrics are available here: <www.jubilate.co.uk/songs/praise_to_the_lord_the_almighty_jubilate_version>.

12. Geraldine Latty, © 2007 Thankyou Music (Admin. by <CapitolCMGPublishing.com> excl. UK & Europe, admin. by Integrity Music, part of the David C. Cook family, <songs@integritymusic.com>). Used by permission.

13. Kreider and Kreider, *Worship and Mission*, p. 135.

14. Frances Ridley Havergal, public domain.

15. For example, Matt Osgood's version available here: <www.resoundworship.org/song/take_my_life>; Geraldine Latty's version available here: <www.geraldinelatty.com/songs/takemylife.htm>.

16. Matt Redman, © 1994 Thankyou Music (Admin. by Integrity Music).

17. Jeffrey J. Taylor, Keith Getty, Kristyn Getty, Stuart Townend, © 2012 Gettymusic (Admin. by Music Services, Inc.), Seek 1st (Admin. by Song Solutions <www.songsolutions.org>), Townend Songs (Admin. by Song Solutions <www. songsolutions.org>).
18. © 1993, 2000, Bernadette Farrell. Published by OCP.
19. Nick Jackson, © 2007 Powerpack (Admin. by amos3music <info@amos3music.com>).
20. John Ellis, © 1997 Thankyou Music (Admin. by Integrity Music).

9. Bible reading

1. Christopher J. Voke, *Creation at Worship: Ecology, Creation and Christian Worship* (Paternoster Press, 2009), p. 129.
2. Alan Kreider and Eleanor Kreider, *Worship and Mission after Christendom* (Paternoster Press, 2009), pp. 141–142.
3. See Robert Webber, *Who Gets to Narrate the World?: Contending for the Christian Story in an Age of Rivals* (IVP, 2008).
4. See Sam and Sara Hargreaves, *How Would Jesus Lead Worship?* (BRF, 2008), pp. 86–87.
5. <engageworship.org/WholeLifeResources>. Also see Bob Hartman, *Telling the Bible* (Monarch, 2006) and *Telling the Gospel* (Monarch, 2010).
6. <www.Taizé.fr/en>.
7. <www.ignatianspirituality.com/ignatian-prayer/the-what-how-why-of-prayer/praying-with-scripture>.
8. Find examples here: <engageworship.org/WholeLifeResources>.
9. Thomas Chisholm, © 1923. Renewed 1951 Hope Publishing Company.
10. Edith McNeill, © 1974, 1975 Celebration.

10. Corporate prayer

1. Mark Greene, *Fruitfulness on the Frontline: Making a Difference Where You Are* (IVP, 2014), p. 189.

2. John Witvliet, 'The Cumulative Power of Transformation in Public Worship', in Alexis D. Abernethy (ed.), *Worship that Changes Lives: Multidisciplinary and Congregational Perspectives on Spiritual Transformation* (Baker Academic, 2008), p. 48.

3. Mark Earey, *Liturgical Worship: A Fresh Look* (Church House Publishing, 2009), p. 9.

4. Luke Hellebronth, Martin Smith, Pete Greig, Tim Hughes, © 2013 Gloworks (Admin. by Integrity Music), Thankyou Music (Admin. by Integrity Music).

5. © 1982, Les Presses de Taizé, GIA Publications, Inc.

6. © Geraldine Latty, <RESOUNDworship.org>, administered by The Jubilate Group. <www.resoundworship.org/song/lord_you_hear_the_cry_lord_have_mercy>.

7. Caroline Bonnett, Sue Rinaldi, © 2014 Sound Travels (Admin. by Song Solutions <www.songsolutions.org>).

8. Sue Rinaldi, interview, 22 February 2016.

9. <engageworship.org/WholeLifeResources>.

10. See Neil Hudson, *Imagine Church: Releasing Whole-Life Disciples* (IVP, 2012), pp. 100–101.

11. <engageworship.org/WholeLifeResources>.

12. Graham Cray, 'Justice, Rock and the Renewal of Worship', in Robin Sheldon (ed.), *In Spirit and in Truth: Exploring Directions in Music in Worship Today* (Hodder and Stoughton, 1989), p. 19.

13. <www.lucemusic.london>.

14. © 2016 Carey and Geraldine Luce.

15. Our favourite one is from Ghana and is published in the songbook *World Praise*.

11. Confession of sin

1. Stanley Hauerwas and Samuel Wells, 'How the Church Managed Before There Was Ethics', in Stanley Hauerwas and Samuel Wells (eds.), *The Blackwell Companion to Christian Ethics* (Blackwell, 2006), p. 449.

2. J. G. Davies, *Worship and Mission* (SCM Press, 1966), p. 127.

3. For an excellent article on the relationship between lives of justice and gathered worship, see Nicholas Wolterstorff, 'Justice as a Condition of Authentic Liturgy', *Theology Today*, vol. 48, no. 1 (1991), pp. 6–21.

4. We recognize that in some traditions only authorized confession texts can be used. You may need to find out from your church leadership what is expected, and work creatively within the frameworks that exist. See Mark Earey, *Finding Your Way Around Common Worship* (Church House Publishing, 2011).

5. Tim Hughes, © 2004 Thankyou Music (Admin. by Integrity Music).

6. Caroline Bonnett, Sue Rinaldi, © 2014 Sound Travels (Admin. by Song Solutions <www.songsolutions.org>).

7. <engageworship.org/WholeLifeResources>.

8. Christopher J. Voke, *Creation at Worship: Ecology, Creation and Christian Worship* (Paternoster Press, 2009), p. 141.

9. Jesse Reeves, Laura Story, © 2004 Laura Stories, sixsteps Music, <worshiptogether.com> songs (Admin. by Capitol CMG Publishing).

10. © 1949 and 1953 Stuart K. Hine Trust (Admin. by Integrity Music).

11. Russell Fragar, © 1998 Hillsong Music Publishing (Admin. by HMTR Limited).

12. Fred Pratt Green, words © 1973 Hope Publishing Company.

13. <engageworship.org/WholeLifeResources>.
14. In some traditions only ordained ministers are permitted to speak words of absolution. Check with your church leadership as to what is expected of you, and work with them to bring creativity and life to these forms.
15. Clayton J. Schmit, *Sent and Gathered: A Worship Manual for the Missional Church* (Baker Academic, 2009), p. 170.
16. Billy J. Foote, © 1996 <worshiptogether.com> songs (Admin. by Capitol CMG Publishing).
17. Chris Tomlin, Louie Giglio, John Newton © 2006 sixsteps Music (Admin. by Capitol CMG Publishing).
18. Rob Hayward, © 1985 Thankyou Music (Admin. by Integrity Music).
19. Davies, *Worship and Mission*, p. 129.
20. Alan Kreider and Eleanor Kreider, *Worship and Mission after Christendom* (Paternoster Press, 2009), p. 154.
21. Graham Kendrick, © 2009 Make Way Music (Admin. by Make Way Music Limited).
22. Mark Thiessen Nation, 'Washing Feet: Preparation for Service', in Hauerwas and Wells (eds.), *The Blackwell Companion*, p. 449.

12. Testimony

1. Neil Hudson, *Imagine Church: Releasing Whole-Life Disciples* (IVP, 2012), p. 46.
2. Chris Tomlin, Ed Cash, Jesse Reeves, © 2004 sixsteps Music (Admin. by Integrity Music), <worshiptogether.com> songs (Admin. by Integrity Music), Wondrously Made Songs (Admin. by Song Solutions <www.songsolutions.org>).
3. Rich Mullins, © 1988 Universal Music – Brentwood Benson Publishing (Admin. by Song Solutions <www.songsolutions.org>).

4. Chris Tomlin, © 2001 sixsteps Music (Admin. by Integrity Music), <worshiptogether.com> songs (Admin. by Integrity Music).

13. Offering

1. John Wimber, 'Why We Worship and the Phases of Worship', *Equipping the Saints*, vol. 1, no. 1, available at <http:// trinityvf.org/wordpress/index.php/2012/12/why-we-worship-the-phases-of-worship-by-john-wimber>.

2. Wimber, 'Why We Worship'.

3. These four are adapted and expanded from four terms used by Christopher Voke: harvest thanks; stewardship; consecration; mission, in his *Creation at Worship: Ecology, Creation and Christian Worship* (Paternoster Press, 2009), pp. 142–143.

4. © 2007 Carol Penner <www.leadinginworship.com>. Used by permission.

5. See also the resources around harvest festivals provided by Hope: <www.hopetogether.org.uk/Groups/256562/Harvest. aspx>.

6. C. Michael Hawn, *Gather into One: Praying and Singing Globally* (Eerdmans, 2003), p. 216.

7. Jan Sutch Pickard, from Neil Paynter (ed.), *50 Great Prayers from the Iona Community* (Wild Goose Publications, 2009), p. 65. Used by permission.

8. Matt Redman, © 1994 Thankyou Music (Admin. by Integrity Music).

9. Isaac Watts, public domain.

10. © Sam Hargreaves / <RESOUNDworship.org>, administered by The Jubilee Group, <www.jubilate.co.uk>. Used by permission. <www.resoundworship.org/song/in_the_light_of_your_mercy>.

11. <www.samaritanspurse.org/what-we-do/operation-christmas-child>.

12. Stephen Burns, *SCM Studyguide: Liturgy* (SCM Press, 2006), p. 19.

13. Rend Collective, © 2011 Thankyou Music (Admin. by Integrity Music).

14. The Lord's Table

1. Clayton J. Schmit, *Sent and Gathered: A Worship Manual for the Missional Church* (Baker Academic, 2009), p. 191.

2. Michael W. Goheen, 'Nourishing Our Missional Identity: Worship and the Mission of God's People', in David J. Cohen and Michael Parsons (eds.), *In Praise of Worship: An Exploration of Text and Practice* (Wipf and Stock, 2010), p. 50.

3. Alan Kreider and Eleanor Kreider, *Worship and Mission after Christendom* (Paternoster Press, 2009), p. 80.

4. Words: William Gadsby; additional lyrics, Jess Alldredge, 2011; music: Jess and Annie Alldredge, 2011, <http://cardiphonia.bandcamp.com/track/feast-on-his-love>.

5. Desmond Tutu, *Hope and Suffering* (Fount, 1983), pp. 134–135, quoted in Graham Cray, 'Justice, Rock and the Renewal of Worship', in Robin Sheldon (ed.), *In Spirit and in Truth: Exploring Directions in Music in Worship Today* (Hodder and Stoughton, 1989), p. 8.

6. Stuart Townend, Phil Baggaley, Mark Edwards, © 2011 Thankyou Music (Admin. by <CapitolCMGPublishing.com> excl. UK & Europe, admin. by Integrity Music, part of the David C. Cook family, <songs@integritymusic.com>), used by permission.

7. Tom Wright, from a talk 'Space, Time and Sacraments (Part 2)' given at Calvin College, 6 January 2007, <http://worship.calvin.edu/resources/resource-library/space-time-

and-sacraments-n-t-wright>. Article version here: <www. reformedworship.org/article/march-2009/nt-wright-word- and-sacraments-eucharist>.

8. Laura Kelly Fanucci, *Everyday Sacrament: The Messy Grace of Parenting* (Liturgical Press, 2014), p. 6.

9. Kreider and Kreider, *Worship and Mission*, p. 53.

10. Tom Wright, from a talk 'Space, Time and Sacraments (Part 1)' given at Calvin College, 6 January 2007, <http:// worship.calvin.edu/resources/resource-library/space-time- and-sacraments-n-t-wright>. Article version here: <www. reformedworship.org/article/september-2008/nt-wright- word-and-sacraments-we-need-both>.

11. From 'Alternative Great Thanksgiving C' available from <www.anglican.org.nz/Resources/Lectionary-and- Worship>. © The Anglican Church in Aotearoa, New Zealand and Polynesia, 2013. Used with permission.

12. Music: Clint Wells, © 2010 Red Mountain Music <http:// redmountainmusic.bandcamp.com/track/all-things-new>.

13. Horatius Bonar (1808–89), public domain.

14. 'Post Communion Prayer' from *Common Worship: Times and Seasons*, © Archbishops' Council, 2006, reproduced by permission of Church House Publishing. <copyright@ churchofengland.org>.

15. Response

1. Bob Rognlien, *Experiential Worship: Encountering God with Heart, Soul, Mind and Strength* (Navpress, 2005), p. 153.

2. Constance M. Cherry, *The Worship Architect: A Blueprint for Designing Culturally Relevant and Biblically Faithful Services* (Baker, 2010), pp. 100–101.

3. For more information on *examen*, visit <www. ignatianspirituality.com/ignatian-prayer/the-examen>.

4. Judson Wheeler Van DeVenter, public domain.
5. © Adam Howard / <RESOUNDworship.org>, administered by The Jubilate Group. <www.resoundworship.org/song/all_i_am_i_lay_it_down>. Reflective video available here: <engageworship.org/WholeLifeResources>.
6. © Joel Payne / <RESOUNDworship.org>, administered by The Jubilate Group, <www.jubilate.co.uk>. Used by permission. <www.resoundworship.org/song/jesus_you_have_called_us>.
7. Scripture is taken from GOD'S WORD®, © 1995 God's Word to the Nations. Used by permission of Baker Publishing Group. This translation uses the word 'by' to show that the singing is instrumental in allowing us to be filled with the Spirit. See Barry Liesch, *The New Worship: Straight Talk on Music and the Church* (Baker, 2001), ch. 2 and appendix 1.
8. Bob Kauflin, 'Why a Synthesizer Isn't the Holy Spirit', <www.worshipmatters.com/2016/03/12/why-a-synthesizer-isnt-the-holy-spirit>.
9. Brenton Brown, Glenn Robertson, © 1998 Vineyard Songs (UK/Eire) (Admin. by Song Solutions, <www.songsolutions.org>).
10. Bryan Torwalt, Katie Torwalt, © 2011 Capitol CMG Genesis (Admin. by Song Solutions, <www.songsolutions.org>), Jesus Culture Music (Admin. by Song Solutions, <www.songsolutions.org>).
11. © 1979 Les Presses de Taizé, admin. GIA Publications, Inc.
12. Edwin Hatch, public domain.
13. William Booth, public domain.
14. Tim Hughes, © 2002 Thankyou Music (Admin. by Integrity Music).
15. Tim Hughes, © 2004 Thankyou Music (Admin. by Integrity Music).

16. As quoted in General Synod of the Church of England, 'Faith, Work and Economic Life' (GS Misc 974B), Education Division, Mission and Public Affairs Division, January 2011.

17. *EG Magazine* (LICC), no. 32 (July 2012), p. 2.

16. Sending

1. Mark Earey, *Liturgical Worship: A Fresh Look* (Church House Publishing, 2009), p. 87.

2. Clayton J. Schmit, *Sent and Gathered: A Worship Manual for the Missional Church* (Baker Academic, 2009), p. 155.

3. Jonas Myrin, Matt Redman, © Thankyou Music (Admin. by Integrity Music). See Matt speak about this song here: <https://youtu.be/pPyudNhfaoE>.

4. Schmit, *Sent and Gathered*, p. 156.

5. For example, John 20:21 and Matthew 28:19–20. Constance M. Cherry covers this at length in her *The Worship Architect: A Blueprint for Designing Culturally Relevant and Biblically Faithful Services* (Baker, 2010), pp. 112–114.

6. Cherry, *The Worship Architect*, p. 115.

7. Mark Earey, interview, 22 February 2016.

8. From *A Wee Worship Book: Fourth Incarnation* (Wild Goose Publications, 1999). Copyright © 1999 WGRG, c/o Iona Community, Glasgow, Scotland. Reproduced by permission. <www.wildgoose.scot>.

9. <engageworship.org/WholeLifeResources>.

10. Words by Charles Wesley (1707–88), public domain. See the contemporary version by Graham Kendrick, © 2008 Make Way Music, <www.grahamkendrick.co.uk/songs/item/61-be-glorified-forth-in-your-name>.

11. Fred Kaan, © 1972 Stainer & Bell Ltd.

12. Martin Leckebusch, © 2010 Kevin Mayhew Ltd. Reproduced by permission of Kevin Mayhew Ltd, Licence no. KMAL040816/01.

13. David Ruis, © 1991 Shade Tree Music (Admin. by Song Solutions), Universal Music – Brentwood Benson Publishing (Admin. by Song Solutions).
14. <engageworship.org/WholeLifeResources>.

17. First steps forward

1. Available from <licc.org.uk/WholeLifeWorship>.
2. Neil Hudson, *Imagine Church: Releasing Whole-Life Disciples* (IVP, 2012), p. 98.
3. <licc.org.uk/WholeLifeWorship>.
4. John Leach. Used by permission. Available with PowerPoint from <engageworship.org/WholeLifeResources>.

INDEX